Mandating the Measurement of Fraud

DOI: 10.1057/9781137406286.0001

Other Palgrave Pivot titles

Colin McInnes, Adam Kamradt-Scott, Kelley Lee, Anne Roemer-Mahler, Owain David Williams and Simon Rushton: The Transformation of Global Health Governance

Tom Watson: Asian Perspectives on the Development of Public Relations: Other Voices

Geir Hønneland: Arctic Politics, the Law of the Sea and Russian Identity: The Barents Sea Delimitation Agreement in Russian Public Debate

Andrew Novak: The Death Penalty in Africa: Foundations and Future Prospects

John Potts: The Future of Writing

Eric Madfis: The Risk of School Rampage: Assessing and Preventing Threats of School Violence

Kevin Jefferys: The British Olympic Association: A History

James E. Will: A Contemporary Theology for Ecumenical Peace

Carrie Dunn: Female Football Fans: Community, Identity and Sexism

G. Douglas Atkins: T.S. Eliot: The Poet as Christian

Raphael Sassower: The Price of Public Intellectuals

Joanne Westwood, Cath Larkins, Dan Moxon, Yasmin Perry and Nigel Thomas: Participation, Citizenship and Intergenerational Relations in Children and Young People's Lives: Children and Adults in Conversation

Jonathan Grix: Leveraging Legacies from Sports Mega-Events: Concepts and Cases

Edward Webb: Media in Egypt and Tunisia: From Control to Transition?

Dayan Jayatilleka: The Fall of Global Socialism: A Counter-Narrative from the South

Linda Lawrence-Wilkes and Lyn Ashmore: The Reflective Practitioner in Professional Education

Anna-Brita Stenström: Teenage Talk: From General Characteristics to the Use of Pragmatic Markers in a Contrastive Perspective

Divya Wodon, Naina Wodon, and Quentin Wodon: Membership in Service Clubs: Rotary's Experience

Robert C. Robinson: Justice and Responsibility—Sensitive Egalitarianism

Alison Heron-Hruby and Melanie Landon-Hays (editors): Digital Networking for School Reform: The Online Grassroots Efforts of Parent and Teacher Activists

R. A. Houston: The Coroners of Northern Britain c. 1300–1700

Christina Slade: Watching Arabic Television in Europe: From Diaspora to Hybrid Citizens

F. E. Knowles, Jr.: The Indian Law Legacy of Thurgood Marshall

Louisa Hadley: Responding to Margaret Thatcher's Death

Kylie Mirmohamadi: The Digital Afterlives of Jane Austen: Janeites at the Keyboard

Rebeka L. Maples: The Legacy of Desegregation: The Struggle for Equality in Higher Education

Stijn Vanheule: Diagnosis and the DSM: A Critical Review

DOI: 10.1057/9781137406286.0001

palgrave▶**pivot**

Mandating the Measurement of Fraud: Legislating against Loss

Martin Tunley

DOI: 10.1057/9781137406286.0001

First published 2014 by
PALGRAVE MACMILLAN

Palgrave Macmillan in the UK is an imprint of Macmillan Publishers Limited, registered in England, company number 785998, of Houndmills, Basingstoke, Hampshire RG21 6XS.

Palgrave Macmillan in the US is a division of St Martin's Press LLC, 175 Fifth Avenue, New York, NY 10010.

Palgrave Macmillan is the global academic imprint of the above companies and has companies and representatives throughout the world.

Palgrave® and Macmillan® are registered trademarks in the United States, the United Kingdom, Europe and other countries

ISBN: 978-1-137-40629-3 EPUB
ISBN: 978-1-137-40628-6 PDF
ISBN: 978-1-137-40627-9 Hardback

This book is printed on paper suitable for recycling and made from fully managed and sustained forest sources. Logging, pulping and manufacturing processes are expected to conform to the environmental regulations of the country of origin.

A catalogue record for this book is available from the British Library.

A catalog record for this book is available from the Library of Congress.

www.palgrave.com/pivot

DOI: 10.1057/9781137406286

Contents

DOI: 10.1057/9781137406286.0001

List of Tables

DOI: 10.1057/9781137406286.0002

DOI: 10.1057/9781137406286.0002

Preface

Existing data suggests that fraud is the most costly crime to society, yet there has been limited academic interest on improving accurate fraud measurement, and no identifiable published research on practitioner and academic opinion on measurement methods and how this process might be improved to generate a more realistic fraud loss figure. This book presents collective opinion on the creation of a standard definition of fraud for measurement purposes, mandating fraud loss measurement drawing upon empirical evidence provided by the United States (US) Improper Payments Information Act 2002, the implementation of a consistent standard of fraud loss measurement, and the development of best practice when measuring fraud losses. The research findings have identified a complacent attitude towards fraud and associated business risks, defined as *immoral phlegmatism*. This publication contributes to the knowledge by offering solutions to address this phenomenon within the public, private and voluntary/charitable sectors. The study conducted is the first of its kind and the project findings have been used to develop recommendations on how to improve the accuracy of fraud loss data through the implementation of the proposed options for change; creating legislation mandating fraud loss measurement in the public and private sectors, the introduction of a British Standard for measuring of fraud, the development of a knowledge exchange infrastructure, and a marketing campaign to increase fraud awareness and associated business risks.

DOI: 10.1057/9781137406286.0003

This book is intended for use by criminologists with an interest in crime measurement, professional public sector readers, policy makers responsible for countering fraud in the public, private and voluntary/charitable sectors, students of fraud and forensic accounting as well as a general readership by introducing them to the concept of fraud and schemes to assess and measure losses resulting from the most costly crime to society.

DOI: 10.1057/9781137406286.0003

List of Abbreviations

ABI	Association of British Insurers
APACS	Association for Payment Clearing Services
BCS	British Crime Survey
BDO	BDO Stoy Hayward
BSI	British Standards Institute
CIFAS	Credit Industry Fraud Avoidance System
DVLA	Driver and Vehicle Licensing Agency
DWP	Department for Work and Pensions
FED	Fraud Error and Debt Taskforce
FSA	Financial Services Authority
HBOS	Halifax Bank of Scotland
HMRC	Her Majesty's Revenue and Customs
IPERA	Improper Payments Elimination and recovery Act of 2010
IPIA	Improper Payments Information Act of 2002
KPMG	Klynveld Peat Marwick Goerdeler
KROLL	Kroll Advisory Solutions
NAO	National Audit Office
NFA	National Fraud Authority
NHS	National Health Service
NHSCFS	NHS Counter Fraud Service
OMB	US Office of Management and Budget
SOX	Sarbanes–Oxley Act 2002

DOI: 10.1057/9781137406286.0004

1
The Issue

Abstract: *Fraud is the most costly crime to society, with estimated losses exceeding those from other acquisitive crimes such as burglary and robbery. However, there have been limited attempts to accurately measure the extent and nature of these losses, which suggests that this figure is only the tip of the iceberg. This chapter introduces the issues addressed within this book by first offering examples of attempts to calculate losses before addressing the question 'what is fraud?' and evidencing that the accurate measurement of fraud is something that is occasionally aspired to but rarely achieved. Examples are then provided of how fraud is measured, and to offer a broader context, a brief review of some measures of corruption is also offered. The focus then moves on to the research argument, followed by a discussion on the value of this research. This chapter then outlines the research methodology, while also discussing the generalizabilty in terms of limitations and scope.*

Tunley, Martin. *Mandating the Measurement of Fraud: Legislating against Loss.* Basingstoke, Palgrave Macmillan, 2014. DOI: 10.1057/9781137406286.0005.

How much does fraud cost?

There are varying estimates of the cost of fraud to the UK, ranging from £7 billion to £73 billion. These annual loss figures include the following: £6.8 billion to £13.8 billion (National Economic Research Associates [NERA], 2000), £16 billion (Norwich Union, 2005), £40 billion (RSM Robson Rodes, 2004) and £72 billion (Mishcon de Reya, 2005). Reviews of these data suggest that losses may range between £14 and £72 billion (Fraud Review Team, 2006; Levi, Burrows, Fleming and Hopkins, 2007). During 2010 annual fraud losses by the public sector, private sector and charities were estimated by the National Fraud Authority (NFA) to be £30.5 billion (NFA, 2010a, p. 8, 2010b, p. 1), increasing in 2012 to an estimated loss of £73 billion (NFA, 2012). Interestingly, the most recent estimation calculates total fraud losses to be £52 billion (NFA, 2013).

Clearly, not all these can be correct; consequently, with such a wide disparity of estimates of the cost of fraud, there is a need for an evaluation of existing measurement methodology to develop a more accurate mechanism which produces meaningful data.

What is fraud?

We have seen how there have been differing attempts to measure fraud and the extreme variations in the loss figures presented. It is therefore relevant to explore what actually constitutes fraud to help to illustrate why there are such wide discrepancies in loss figures. Historically, that is to say prior to the Fraud Act 2006, one of the most frequently asked questions was 'what is fraud?' The collective academic and practitioner response being that there was no 'definitive' or 'universal' definition (Doig, Johnson and Levi, 2001; Fraud Advisory Panel, 1999). This lack of a universal definition has significantly limited any meaningful measurement of fraud. The consequence being that organizations apply their own bespoke definition which restricts any meaningful analysis and comparability. The Fraud Advisory Panel's (1999) study of published literature on fraud identifies only one report offering a definition of fraud (p. 6), this being 'the use of deception with the intention of obtaining advantage, avoiding an obligation or causing loss to a third party' (Her Majesty's Treasury, 1995, p. 6). This definition, while being rather dated, does summarize the key elements of the Fraud Act 2006 and warrants consideration when developing a standard definition for measurement purposes, being both succinct and unambiguous.

The aim of the Fraud Act 2006 is to simplify matters and improve general understanding of this crime. According to the legislation fraud can be perpetrated in three clearly defined ways:

- ▸ By false representation.
- ▸ By abuse of position.
- ▸ By failure to disclose.

The statute does offer a description of how fraud is committed; however, it fails to answer the definitional question of what actually constitutes fraud.

Optimistically, Hoare (2007) argues that this statute facilitates 'effective measurement of fraud' by making 'recording and reporting fraud easier' (p. 277). While being of relevance to this research, this view is based on the presumption that fraud losses may only be measured using reported or detected data, which is no longer the case.

Unfortunately, this legislation has failed to address the problem of multiple definitions of fraud, because 'drafting for legal purposes seldom provides ... behavioural categorisation that corresponds to the way individuals and businesses categorise frauds' (Levi et al., 2007, p. 9). This observation being evidenced by the continuing range of fraud definitions used for measurement purposes following the introduction of this statute (Audit Commission, 2013; Levi and Burrows, 2008). The latter defining fraud as 'any intentional false representation, including failure to declare information or abuse of position that is carried out to make gain, cause loss or expose another to the risk of loss' (Audit Commission, 2013, p. 8). This exemplifies two important common themes required within a universal definition, these being financial gain and causing loss.

The civil definition of fraud, Derry v Peek (1889), considers fraud to have been proved 'when it is shown that a false representation has been made (a) knowingly, or (b) without belief in its truth, or (c) recklessly, careless whether it be true or false'. The burden of proof is based on the balance of probabilities rather than 'beyond reasonable doubt', thus if applied for measurement purposes would include cases where fraud is identified but with insufficient evidence for a criminal prosecution. Accordingly, it offers a potential option as a standard fraud definition for the purpose of more accurate loss measurement.

DOI: 10.1057/9781137406286.0005

Why do we measure crime and fraud?

It is also worth considering why crime and fraud are actually measured. Foucault (1977, 1979, 2000) argues that collecting information about individuals forms part of a government strategy to extend control over the population. Levi and Burrows (2008, p. 293) make a similar observation, suggesting that the collection of crime data 'to serve the panoptican poses a question, namely answers are required concerning what is required and what is not collected by those managing the state'. This suggests there may be a political agenda in terms of data collection, and explanations are required as to why on occasions the state fails to look too closely at certain crime types. Brand and Price (2000, p. 3) offer a simple explanation for the collection of crime data, suggesting that it provides a way of measuring crime reduction policies. Accordingly, a precise representation of fraud losses enables focused investment in, and deployment of, any tactical counter-fraud resource.

Do we really look for fraud?

It has been suggested that policies encouraging individuals to report fraud may result in an unachievable public expectation on law enforcement agencies to address this issue (Levi and Burrows, 2008, p. 315). To alleviate such a risk, it may be in the interest of law enforcement agencies and the government to undercount fraud, which may explain limited interest in fraud loss measurement.

It is therefore worthwhile considering why these data are collected, and possible motives for not looking too hard. The Home Office has been criticized for targeting research to suit the government's political agenda (Walters, 2005, p. 6). This charge may also be levelled at the collection, or in some cases lack of collection, by central government departments of fraud loss data. In support of this contention, this book offers the findings of a public sector fraud survey which reveals that in the preceding 12 months, only 52 per cent of government-owned enterprises reported economic crime (PriceWaterhouseCoopers, 2010).

Insurance companies pose another dilemma, frequently absorbing losses because fraud is seen as a consequence of a high volume of transactions. This suggests that fraud is considered a business cost by these organizations, and therefore should be measured accurately. Reluctance to confront this issue by the private sector due to fear of organizational embarrassment, or in the case of the charitable sector, concerns that exposure may impact on donations and may explain the limited engagement with fraud loss measurement by these sectors. Limited appreciation of the amount of potential losses to fraud may also result in these organizations believing it may be more cost effective to ignore rather than address the issue.

How do we measure fraud?

There are different mechanisms for measuring fraud used by both the public and private sectors offering varying levels of accuracy and statistical confidence. These include:

▸ (Censuses drawing on) administrative records of fraud reports.
▸ Probability and non-probability sample surveys of individuals and firms as fraud victims.
▸ Audits of probability samples of customers/accounts/transactions/ expenditures to uncover fraud losses.
▸ Analyses of samples of Suspicious Activity Reports filed on suspicion of money laundering.
▸ Analyses of samples of offenders convicted of certain frauds or of law enforcement case information.

(Fleming, 2009, p. 11)

This array of methods explains why there is a range of estimates of the true cost of fraud, and evidences an urgent need to apply a more consistent approach to loss measurement.

An additional factor impacting upon the calculation of fraud losses and offering an explanation for the variety of measures is cost. The amount of resources devoted to measurement exercises influences the reliability and statistical confidence of resultant data. Limited resources may result in sporadic measurement exercises, with insufficient samples which subsequently generate unreliable data that offers limited scope for developing cost-effective control strategies. To address this problem there is a pressing requirement to change the way in which fraud losses are viewed. They must be treated as a business cost and measured accordingly.

DOI: 10.1057/9781137406286.0005

Measuring corruption

There is sometimes a blurring of the edges between fraud and corruption. For example, fraud by those holding a position of trust may also constitute corruption. The measurement of fraud and corruption do pose different challenges (Samford, Shacklock, Connors and Galtung, 2006); however there is some overlap. Accordingly, it is worth reviewing some measures of corruption to offer a broader contextualization of the measurement of crimes that are covert by nature. There are a wide range of corruption measures worldwide, and this chapter confines itself to a small sample to illustrate that, similar to fraud, differing measurement methodologies exist. Furthermore, similar to fraud, there is a myth that corruption cannot be measured. This is incorrect; corruption can be and is being measured through a wide variety of innovative approaches (Kaufman, Kraay and Mastruzzi, 2006, p. 5). There are two typologies of corruption measures that this evaluation will focus on, these being qualitative and quantitative by nature. The review will commence by exploring perception surveys before moving on to consider some of the quantitative measures. For the purpose of this evaluation, corruption is defined as 'the misuse of power in the interest of illicit gain' (Anderson and Heywood, 2009, p. 748).

Transparency International's *Corruption Perceptions Index* was first produced in 1995 and draws upon multiple data sources to calculate the extent of corruption by country, currently 117 countries and territories. In fact 13 data sources were used to construct the 2013 index, including World Bank, World Economic Forum, Economist Intelligence Unit and Political and Economic Risk Consultancy. These datasets were collected in differing years ranging from 2011 to 2014. This survey only measures perceptions, and there is no standard definition of corruption as each of the incorporated surveys operates with its own understanding. Each survey may focus on different aspects of corruption such as bribery of public officials or embezzlement for example. No statistical data such as prosecutions, reported cases or proven incidents of corruption are included. Furthermore, historically the number of participating countries has varied, and thus a country's position in the table could be influenced by how many countries are covered in any one year. However, since the 2012 index, a revised scoring system has been introduced based on a scale of 0–100 which will be used year on year thus allowing comparison and longitudinal analysis. The significant limitation of

DOI: 10.1057/9781137406286.0005

these data is that they are based on opinion which can be influenced by a number of factors including media reporting of high profile cases and the number of corruption prosecutions. Accordingly, there can be a significant difference between perceptions and the true level of corruption in any country, and the report should be treated as a measure of corruption perceptions and not corruption itself (Rohwer, 2009, p. 51).

The World Bank offers a similar index, known as the *Control of Corruption Indicator*, which was first produced in 1999. The methodology employed is similar to that of Transparency International, drawing upon many of the same sources of data. In fact, of the 22 data sources Transparency International used for their index during the period 2002–2007, 13 were used by World Bank for this index (Hawken and Munck, 2009). Again, this should be treated as a measure of perceptions and not as a robust measure of corruption itself. Furthermore, many of the data sources used are selected to further organizational business interests (Hawken and Munck, 2009, p. 5), and thus may offer a biased view.

Another perception is the *Global Corruption Barometer* (Transparency International, 2013) which seeks to capture the experiences, rather than opinions, of individuals in 107 countries, and how corruption features in their everyday lives. The survey 'addresses people's direct experience with bribery and details their views on corruption in the main institutions in their countries' (p. 3). These data may offer a measure on the instances of corruption, but cannot offer a reliable and statistically valid measure of costs.

The *International Crime and Victims Survey* has been conducted six times during the period 1989–2010. The data are gathered through the distribution of a questionnaire which facilitates international comparability. The most recent survey was conducted in 13 countries (Van Dijk, 2012). Later surveys have included corruption; with respondents being asked if government officials, such as police officers, had solicited or expected bribes for services during the last year. However, the survey does not ask respondents whether they actually paid and is more about the experience of 'attempted extortion' (Miller, 2006, p. 169), rather than a reliable measure of corruption.

This chapter now considers quantitative measures which evidence that, similar to fraud, a monetary value can be placed on financial losses resulting from corruption. The first methodology considered is *Public Expenditure Tracking Surveys*, which are project-based and track the movement of resources, usually through government bureaucracy until

DOI: 10.1057/9781137406286.0005

it reaches the service facilities it is intended to fund. A typical survey 'consists of a survey of frontline providers (schools and clinics and their staff) and local governments (politicians and public officials)', supplemented by central government financial data (Reinikka and Svensson, 2005, p. 360). This type of metric is essential because it monitors 'aid programs and reconstruction processes' (United Nations Development Programme, 2008, p. 12). However, the drawback is that an exercise such as this is very expensive to perform.

A further corruption measure within this typology is a *Quantitative Service Delivery Survey*. This variation of a frontline provider survey examines 'finances, inputs, outputs, pricing, quality, oversight and other aspects of service provision' (Reinikka and Svensson, 2005, p. 363). This survey often involves multiple data collection techniques including harvesting quantitative data 'from facility records' and 'interviews with staff' (Amin and Chaudhury, 2008, p. 82). The advantage of this type of measure is that it can be applied across public, private and not for profit sectors and generates useful data on corrupt practices within service delivery.

From the evidence presented it is clear that, similar to fraud, there are a range of corruption measures and there are also comparable issues in terms of data quality. The use of perception surveys realistically only supplies data on individual opinion and thus only measures the level of perceived or suspected corruption, rather than actual levels. On a positive note, there is evidence that corruption can be measured, and through the use of quantitative data surveys, an actual estimated monetary figure of losses can be achieved. The myth that corruption cannot be measured has been disproved and this can actually be used to evidence that if it is possible to measure corruption, which may be considered even more deceptive than fraud, then the arguments that fraud can be measured more accurately hold more credence.

Research argument and significance

Fraud is a serious crime and deserves the equivalent attention that is paid to other acquisitive crimes. A 2003–2004 Home Office survey of crime against individuals and households estimated the total cost to be £36.2 billion, of which £2.1 billion represented the value of property stolen (Home Office, 2005, p. 15). However, this research failed to include fraud within any calculations. The most recent Annual Fraud Indicator

DOI: 10.1057/9781137406286.0005

estimates fraud losses experienced by individuals at £9.1 billion (NFA, 2013, p. 24). Even allowing for inflation, fraud losses are approximately three times greater than those resulting from all other volume property crimes. Turning our attention to businesses, there is an even larger difference between losses to volume crime and fraud. The last estimate by the NFA (2013, pp. 11–12) puts the total cost of fraud losses against organizations at £52 billion. This compares to a figure of £4.2 billion for the calculated value of property stolen from commercial and public sector organizations when last estimated by the Home Office (Brand and Price, 2000). Similarly, even when taking inflation into account, the significant size of the problem is illustrated when comparing fraud losses with those from other volume crimes. We can therefore conclude that fraud is the most costly crime to society, and therefore developing a more accurate measure warrants careful consideration.

Since fraud is a recurring problem, it requires 'continuous monitoring and assessment' (Brooks, Button and Frimpong, 2009, p. 497); however there is minimal guidance on how to accurately measure fraud losses, resulting in limited empirical evaluation of the true cost. This book argues that it is no longer acceptable to continue with the assumption that fraud losses cannot be quantified accurately. There are existing fraud loss data outputs; however these are of limited rigour, drawing upon a variety of measurement methodologies, many relying solely on perception, which are nothing more than guesstimates. These studies also employ varying definitions of fraud and frequently only measure detected cases. Thus when taking account of the low detection rate of many law enforcement agencies, these data only scratch the surface when attempting to paint a true and accurate picture of fraud losses.

The existing literature evaluating the accuracy of fraud loss data concludes that existing measures lack credibility, having been based on a variety of different methods (Fraud Review Team, 2006; Hoare, 2007; Levi et al., 2007; Levi and Burrows, 2008). However, these bodies of knowledge fail to address the issue of improving accuracy, and therefore minimal progress has been made in developing a more robust measure of fraud.

A more accurate measure of fraud will also contribute to crime reduction, this being achieved by multiple policies working in tandem (Walker, 2011, p. 8). Adopting a policy of regularly measuring and re-measuring fraud losses to an improved standard of accuracy, and using the resultant data to reduce vulnerability through informed prevention policies can lead to a reduction in fraudulent criminal activity.

DOI: 10.1057/9781137406286.0005

Empirical evidence that this is achievable is provided by the National Health Service (NHS), which between 1998 and 2006 conducted regular statistically valid fraud loss measurement exercises, with the resultant data informing fraud reduction strategies. As a consequence of this strategy fraud losses were reduced by up to 60 per cent (Gee and Helwig, 2008, p. 19). If this large fragmented organization can develop and implement such a process, then it is not beyond the capabilities of central and local government and even private sector organizations to develop something similar. Once established, progress on achieving crime reduction can be gauged by regular re-measurement exercises.

Adopting regular measurement exercises also offers financial value to organizations by treating fraud losses as a business cost and taking appropriate remedial action (Gee, 2009a, 2009b). This may then result in 'greater pressures from shareholders, taxpayers, governing bodies to reduce this cost' (Button, Johnston and Frimpong, 2008, p. 246). Moreover, implementation of a robust fraud loss measurement process by large organizations may then encourage smaller organizations to fund similar measurement exercises. Equally, if adequate investment is made in fraud measurement, 'a considerable return' that actually exceeds the cost of such exercises is achievable (Gee, 2007, p. 7), simply because limited focus upon fraud costs means they have become one of the 'great unreduced business costs' (Gee, 2010a, p. 13). The financial value of re-measurement is also worthy of consideration. When reviewing statistically valid fraud loss measurement exercises, Button, Gee and Brooks (2012, p. 71) identified that organizations repeating fraud loss measurement exercises tended to show a reduction in the percentage loss rate, equating to an average of just below 15 per cent, which in many organizations 'would amount to a significant sum of money'.

The limited attention paid to fraud measurement has informed the research argument. Accordingly, this publication advocates that there is an urgent need to develop a consistent standard of fraud measurement, supported by best practice guidance.

This book argues that this is achievable through the following options for change:

▸ mandating the measurement of fraud
▸ creating a British Standard of fraud measurement to support the statute which incorporates a universal definition of fraud for measurement purposes

DOI: 10.1057/9781137406286.0005

> implementing a knowledge-exchange infrastructure that develops core doctrine through the establishment of a 'manual of guidance'.

Method selection

According to Kaplan (1964, p. 23) methodology assists the understanding of the processes of scientific enquiry. Data were required to measure opinion on the research argument, while also seeking individual and organizational perspectives on fraud measurement. Selecting the most appropriate technique for measuring opinion, while also maintaining rigour, was imperative. To evaluate the viability of the research argument, I concluded that the topic under investigation required the collection of rich empirical data from multiple sources to complement each other.

First, the views of fraud professionals and academics contributing to the literature on fraud were required on the research argument. This was to ascertain whether the research argument was viable in its entirety, or required any revisions. The second strand of the research sought data from a larger sample of individuals involved in fraud investigation, fraud measurement or audit from a range of organizations, acting as a barometer of opinion 'from the field' on the research argument. Having considered the appropriate sample size for each data source, it became apparent that qualitative methodology was appropriate for the first strand of data collection because of the detailed informed opinion required on the research argument (Denscombe, 2010, p. 152). Whereas, the volume of data required for the second research component to ensure validity suggested that this paradigm was not appropriate (Nardi, 2006, p. 17). Accordingly, a pragmatic decision was taken to mix methods, blending quantitative and qualitative strategies into a single study (Morse, 2003, p. 191).

Collecting data

Structured interviews using predetermined questions were conducted because they were considered the most suitable method of obtaining the qualitative data required, and permitted comparison of responses. The

DOI: 10.1057/9781137406286.0005

interviews were designed as conversations 'with a purpose' (Kahn and Canell, 1957, p. 149) to extract the empirical data required.

To obtain a 'snapshot' of extant attitudes to fraud measurement in the empirical setting, and to ensure a representative sample of organizations within the public, private and charitable sectors, an electronically issued questionnaire was considered the apposite quantitative data collection methodology. The sampling frame for organizations within the target population was easily obtainable from websites containing electronic lists of central government departments, local authorities, the FTSE 100 and 250 companies and charities.

Since the identity of the individuals responsible for managing fraud or internal audit was unknown, a covering letter was sent by email to the chief executive of each organization. This requested that they act as 'gatekeeper' by forwarding the questionnaire web link to the person within the organization most qualified to respond. Where the chief executive's contact details were unavailable, the request was issued to the most appropriate email address found on the organization's website. Each email sent requested a 'delivery receipt' to confirm it had reached the intended recipient organization. The resultant data has ensured that this is the largest survey to date on this subject, thus providing a starting point for the development of new knowledge.

Limitations in research scope

It is important to note that there are inherent limitations in this type of study. It was important to obtain the views of academics with knowledge of fraud measurement or the impact of fraud in the UK. However, since this is a topic receiving limited academic attention there was only a small pool of potential interviewees. Having identified potential interviewees, the criteria determining selection was willingness to participate and availability for interview. Consequently, those interviewed may not be considered totally representative of all academic opinion within this field. Nevertheless, I am satisfied that those interviewed fully understood the research subject, having all published on fraud losses or fraud loss measurement, and were able to provide valuable data, which helped establish an evidence base on the feasibility of this study and the data required from the questionnaire. The remaining six interviewees were fraud professionals involved in

DOI: 10.1057/9781137406286.0005

fraud loss measurement. Being a small sample, their views may not be fully representative of the entire Counter Fraud Specialist population; however, they offered valuable informed opinion on the research argument from a practitioner perspective.

I also acknowledge there are limitations with the data from the survey, in terms of representation of the broader population. I do not claim these data to be totally representative, rather a 'barometer of opinion' that may reflect the views of the wider counter-fraud specialist population.

Book outline

This book comprises of seven chapters. Chapter 2 discusses the three proposed options for change to improve the accuracy of fraud measurement in more detail.

The subject of fraud measurement is taken up in Chapter 3, initially by introducing the concept of the dark figure of fraud, before conducting a thematic literature review that offers an overview of the existing limited critiques of fraud measurement, before moving on to evaluate existing fraud loss data outputs. The purpose of this chapter is to evaluate existing measurement methodologies, with a view to identify best practice and inadequacies of measurement techniques.

Chapters 4–6 describe the research findings, addressing the topics of who measures fraud and the methods applied, mandating fraud measurement, the creation of a common standard of fraud measurement and the development of doctrine.

Chapter 7 summarizes the entire book by offering conclusions based on the analysis of data collected and recommendations that offer improvements to existing practice.

Review

This chapter has discussed the historical difficulties in defining fraud, and how lack of a universally applied definition has hampered accurate and consistent measurement, before detailing some of the varying definitions that have been applied. The evidence presented however suggests that to progress these proposed changes, a standard definition

DOI: 10.1057/9781137406286.0005

of fraud is the starting point. Examples have been provided of the ways in which both fraud and corruption are measured. This chapter has also outlined the research argument and introduced the proposed options for change, these being mandating fraud measurement, creating a British Standard of fraud measurement and creating a knowledge-exchange infrastructure.

DOI: 10.1057/9781137406286.0005

2
Options for Change

Abstract: *This research project has identified three options to address the issue of a significant lack of accurate and consistent fraud loss measurement data, and a restricted knowledge base on fraud risk and the financial benefits of accurate fraud loss measurement. These being: mandating the measurement of fraud through legislation, the creation of a British Standard of fraud measurement and the establishment of a knowledge exchange infrastructure to develop core doctrine of fraud loss measurement and promote best practice.*

Tunley, Martin. *Mandating the Measurement of Fraud: Legislating against Loss*. Basingstoke, Palgrave Macmillan, 2014. DOI: 10.1057/9781137406286.0006.

Mandating the measurement of fraud

The increased prevalence of fraud and error in the United States (US) led to Government intervention mandating its measurement in certain public bodies through the Improper Payments Information Act (IPIA) of 2002 (Button, Gee and Brooks, 2012, p. 69; Tunley, 2010a). During fiscal year (FY) 2000, the federal government of the US spent approximately $1.8 trillion and has a responsibility to the taxpayer to safeguard against improper payments (United States General Accounting Office, 2001, p. 1). Improper payments are defined as 'any payments that should not have been made or that were made in an incorrect amount under statutory, contractual, administrative, or other legally applicable requirement' (Gordon and Willox, Jr, 2005, p. 2; United States Office of Management and Budget [US OMB], 2006, p. 2). These incorrectly issued payments are a significant issue, receiving increased attention by the federal government (United States General Accounting Office, 2001, p. 7). For example, the President's Management Agenda for 2002 advocated direct action to improve performance. The resultant IPIA of 2002 requires all Federal agencies to 'annually review programs and activities they administer, identify those that may be susceptible to improper payments, and submit a report on actions taken to reduce improper payments' (Schick, 2007, p. 297). Each agency is also required to report on the capability of their current information systems and infrastructure to support the effort to reduce improper payments.

Agencies are required to systematically review all their programs and identify any 'annual erroneous payments in the program exceeding both 2.5 per cent of the program payments and $10 million' (US OMB, 2003, p. 2). Agencies must also estimate annual losses by conducting a random sample large enough to yield an estimate with a 90 per cent confidence interval within 5 per cent precision, develop and implement plans to reduce these erroneous payments and report these figures to the president through the Office of Management and Budget and Congress (Hatch and McMurtry, 2009, p. 3). A further important development has been the development of sampling methodologies appropriate to individual agency requirements, thus improving statistical validity.

Each Federal Agency is responsible for conducting loss measurement exercises and reporting these findings to the OMB either in the Agency's Performance and Accountability Report or Annual Financial Report. Compliance with the IPIA is policed using each individual

DOI: 10.1057/9781137406286.0006

agency's Inspectors General, who are politically independent individuals appointed under the Inspector General Act 1978, and responsible for ensuring agency compliance with legislation by conducting financial audits of the agency's IPIA reporting. Each agency Inspector General verifies publication of improper payment data, and that the agency has conducted a risk assessment for each program identified as meeting the criteria laid down in the statute (Federal Housing Finance Agency Office of Inspector General, 2013).

To assist implementation, guidance has been created to improve the management of improper payments. Agencies are required to systematically review all their programs and identify those at risk to significant improper payments. Re-measurement is also an important part of the process, this providing information on the effectiveness of the control activities put in place and assisting identification of areas requiring further attention.

There has been renewed focus on improper payments by the Obama administration, which were reported at $100 billion for FY 2009 (US OMB, 2010, p. 1). While these figures may still be inflated due to the credit crunch, an Executive Order signed by the President on 20 November 2009 aims to reduce improper payments through increased transparency of the process. In the wake of the economic downturn it would not be unreasonable to accept an increase in fraud, however, the continued determination of the US Government to reduce fraud is creditable, and a policy the UK government should embrace with similar tangible actions rather than just rhetoric.

To supplement the IPIA, on 22 July 2010 the Improper Payments Elimination and Recovery Act of 2010 (IPERA) became public law. The statute redefines 'significant' in terms of dollar levels, and from FY 2013 onwards, requires improper payments which amount to 1.5 per cent or more of total outlays of $100 million or more to be reported. This supplementary legislation has led to an increase in measurement, resulting in a more accurate picture of the extent of losses. The statute also requires agency heads to conduct recovery audits for all programs that spend $1 million or more annually, and permits agencies to retain up to 25 per cent of funds recovered, thus incentivizing increased fraud loss measurement activity.

In March 2010, as a precursor to IPERA, President Obama announced a further initiative to recover improper payments identified through measurement. These being payment recapture audits, which employ private sector auditors to examine government payments and recover those identified as fraudulently claimed. Accordingly, the implementation of the IPIA and the subsequent IPERA has had a significant impact on measuring and reducing improper payments. Regular measuring and implementation of remedial action has resulted in a continued decrease in the improper payment rate for all programs that commenced measurement between 2004 and 2007, this falling from 4.3 per cent in FY 2004 to 2.8 per cent in FY 2008. Despite this progress, Hatch and McMurtry (2009, p. 9) are somewhat critical, arguing that 'nearly one third (31%) of the programs in the FY 2004 cohort ... have seen no improvement in their error rates after five years of improper payments reporting'. When viewed from a different position however, these data suggest that over two-thirds have demonstrated an improvement in their error rates. This is an admirable achievement, particularly when compared with the UK public sector experience. The Department for Work and Pensions (DWP) commenced fraud measurement in 1997, yet it was not until 2004–2005, that changes in measurement methodology improved the accuracy of data (National Audit Office, 2008a).

Additional programs commenced measurement in 2008, and as a consequence, the government-wide improper payment rate increased to 5.42 per cent in FY 2009, before decreasing to 4.35 per cent in 2012. The United States Government Accountability Office (2012) also reports that 50 per cent of the programs reporting improper payments in FY 2011, declared a reduction in the error rate. Additionally, federal agencies reported a decrease in improper payments of $5.3 billion for FY 2011 compared to the previous year's figures. Further improvements were reported the following year, with President Obama announcing that the Administration would avoid $50 billion in improper payments by the end of FY 2012.

Published results also indicate a positive impact in recovering the debt resulting from improper payments. This is evidenced by the fact that, by the end of FY 2012 the US Government recovered $4.4 billion worth of improper payments made to contractors. These results demonstrate the positive impact of mandating fraud loss measurement and setting recovery targets through the creation of legislation, and I contend that this is an option for change worthy of consideration when trying to improve the extent, quality and cost effectiveness of fraud loss measurement within the United Kingdom (UK).

When evaluating mandating fraud measurement in the private sector, the area that gives cause for concern is the banking sector, where a

DOI: 10.1057/9781137406286.0006

reluctance to supply mortgage fraud data resulted in an undercounting of banking fraud (National Fraud Authority [NFA], 2010a). There is also a likelihood that losses may be recovered through increased costs passed on to the consumer. It is therefore worth considering the inclusion of the banking industry in any proposal. Furthermore, the revelation that insurance companies make good their fraud losses by increased premiums (Association of British Insurers [ABI], 2009) suggests that this industry is also worthy of consideration for incorporation into any proposed statute. Interestingly, the US also offers an example of where persuasion has been unsuccessful, and it has been necessary for the state to intervene and regulate the insurance industry. As a result, a statute was created whereby each organization is legally required to form and maintain a fraud special investigation unit and monitor its performance.

I do however offer one caveat to this recommendation, this being that the proposed exercises based upon statistically valid samples are only applicable to 'a relatively homogenous group of transactions' including 'payroll, procurement, housing, education grant payments, social security and tax credit payments, healthcare payments, insurance claims, pensions, agriculture subsidy payments and compensation claims' (Button and Gee, 2013, p. 74).

A British Standard of fraud measurement

In 1999 the Council of Standards Australia and New Zealand prepared and adopted a joint standard on risk management to provide a cultural framework for managing risk to minimize losses, including fraud. In the UK, the British Standards Institution (BSI) underpins the development and maintenance of best practice through the publication of British Standards, of which there are 27,000. Following such a code of practice provides assurance that an organization has parity with international best practices, while also providing 'a single reference point' (von Solms, 2000, p. 617). To comply with such a standard, and display the British Standard logo, 'procedures have to be established and then documented; staff trained to follow procedures' (Mistry and Usherwood, 1996, p. 1). The process is then measured 'using performance indicators and evaluated against predetermined standards; and the firm audited by a recognized external body' (Mistry and Usherwood, 1996, p. 1).

DOI: 10.1057/9781137406286.0006

While monitoring and evaluation may be an extended procedure, it ensures that the process is performed to a consistently high standard, and also offers the opportunity to compare data between organizations, or to conduct longitudinal studies. Therefore, to ensure consistent fraud measurement to a prescribed level of accuracy, a further option for change is the creation of a British Standard of fraud measurement. There are already British and International standards for auditing and accounting. For example, BS 6001-5:2002/ISO 2859-4 provides guidance on sampling procedures appropriate for reviews or audits (British Standards Institute, 2002, p. v). Similarly, BS 600:2000 provides guidance on statistical methods 'applicable to administrative areas and to all sectors including commerce and public service' (British Standards Institute, 2000, p. x). Additionally, the Auditing Practices Board (2010) produces an international standard outlining an auditor's responsibilities relating to fraud when auditing financial statements, however this only advocates that an auditor should consider the possibility of fraud and offers no guidance on measurement. These documents do however offer a useful starting point to inform the development of a British Standard of fraud loss measurement.

Information exchange matrix

To support the implementation of mandating legislation, the US Government has established working groups that exchange relevant information concerning the measurement of improper payments and the development of good practice (United States General Accounting Office, 2001). The third option being considered therefore is the structured and controlled sharing of best practice between organizations. This could include successful data collection and analysis methodologies which could be documented within a manual of guidance. This exchange of information could be implemented through the creation of a best practice database supplemented by the creation of a fraud measurement working group populated by fraud measurement champions from all sectors. To progress this option, it is important that 'the required infrastructure is in place' which forms part of a 'wider knowledge management strategy' (Reddy and McCarthy, 2006, p. 597). A possible conduit for such an infrastructure is a panel of academic experts, such as those currently involved in externally reviewing the National Fraud Authority's Annual

DOI: 10.1057/9781137406286.0006

Fraud Indicator (NFA, 2012, p. 6). It is also vital that this information exchange matrix remains in after the creation of a statute mandating fraud measurement to develop core doctrine.

Justifying state intervention

When evaluating whether there is a need for state intervention, it is initially worth contextualizing the scale and cost of fraud within all criminal activity against individuals and organizations to evidence the impact of this offending typology. Statistical data suggests that crime trends have continued to reduce since 2003, however, even allowing for inflation, as discussed in Chapter 1, fraud losses are in the region of four times greater than from other crimes. This statistic illustrates the significant size of the fraud problem in comparison to other crimes; specifically that fraud is the most costly crime to society, and thus state intervention is a justifiable consideration.

Past governments have used Keynesian ideas to justify state intervention (Aaronovitch, 1983, p. 46; Gunn, 2004, p. 117). Arguably, the labour government also drew upon Keynesian principles to justify a 'bailout' during the banking crisis. The rescue of Northern Rock by means of government intervention was described by Gordon Brown as 'action that was necessary' (Hencke and Sparrow, 2009, p. 1). Previously, during September 2007, £24 billion in emergency loans had been authorized to be paid to Northern Rock, justified by the Chancellor because 'the government has an interest in maintaining financial stability' (Politics. co.uk, 2007, p. 1). There seemed no end to state intervention, in October 2008 the government took a £37 billion stake in three banks, Royal Bank of Scotland, Lloyds TSB and HBOS (Channel Four News, 2009, p. 1). Further loans authorized in January 2009 were justified by the Prime Minister on the grounds that 'good businesses must have access to credit' (Livingstone, 2009, p. 1). When reflecting upon the labour government's interventions, it is worth comparing the value of the losses with fraud loss figures. For example the proposed losses at HBOS, forecast to be 'nearly £11 billion' (British Broadcasting Corporation, 2009, p. 1) fall well below the total of £17.6 billion lost to fraud by the public sector during 2008 (NFA, 2010a, p. 1).

In 2009 the Government provisionally estimated that net losses from its financial sector interventions may lie between £20 billion

DOI: 10.1057/9781137406286.0006

and £50 billion (House of Commons Treasury Committee, 2009). The Committee also concluded that the government 'was right to take decisive action in response to the exceptional instability in financial markets' (House of Commons Treasury Committee, 2009, p. 6). Here it is worth revisiting the NFA's (2010a) Annual Fraud Indicator, which estimates 2008 public sector fraud losses at £17.6 billion. When also considering the potential for undercounting by central government departments, then the true loss figure may be even closer to the lower limit of the projected losses from the banking crisis. Applying the average fraud loss figure of 5.7 per cent, calculated by reviewing 205 statistically valid fraud loss measurement exercises from nine countries (Button and Gee, 2013, p. 73) to UK public sector expenditure of almost £600 billion, the resultant losses would equate to £34 billion, thus far exceeding the £20 billion projected losses from bailing out the banks. I suggest that escalating public sector fraud losses, and a requirement to address the 'black holes in the budget' (Trickett, 2010, p. 2), are compelling arguments for the state to intervene and mandate the measurement of fraud. The argument is made even more persuasive by evidence that regular accurate measurement exercises, and use of the resultant data to inform control strategies, contribute to reducing these losses, and in the case of the NHS, offer a 12:1 return on the cost of the work (Gee, 2009a, p. 20).

When exploring the justification for state intervention further, the principal consideration is 'will the recommended government intervention have the desired impact?' (Belli, 1997, p. 2). Clearly in the current macro-economic climate with significant spending cuts, mandating fraud measurement warrants serious consideration. Particularly, when evidence from the NHS supports the contention that regular measurement exercises reduce loss by up to 40 per cent within the first year (Button and Gee, 2013, p. 187), and that 'taken as a proportion of the measured losses, this equates to two per cent being added to the "bottom line" within a year' (Gee, 2010a, p. 13).

Accordingly, there is scope for pragmatic state intervention (Adams, 2001, p. 29), thus ensuring the provision of accurate fraud data, rather than a free market where individual choice prevails. Moreover, it could be suggested the government are morally obliged to intervene to fulfil their role as 'the guardian of equity and the interests of future generations' (Arrow, 1978, p. ix). Therefore, by mandating the measurement of fraud in the interest of 'social justice' (Fan, 2008, p. 5), state intervention would be justified by reducing the loss of public funds which in turn may contribute to a 'net increase in social welfare' (International Monetary Fund, 2000, p. 176) by limiting the cuts in public spending.

When debating state intervention into the private sector, it is worth returning to the previously discussed 'government bailout' during the banking crisis. The need for such action has been attributed to 'the problems in performance of subprime mortgages in the United States' (Hellwig, 2008, p. 3), which was certainly built upon negligence, if not a great deal of fraud. This all culminated in creating a growth in mortgages, which were doomed for default (Bitner, 2008; Ferguson, 2008). The case for state intervention can be further evidenced by the global impact of this subprime mortgage crisis on both financial institutions and wider society.

The cost of this resultant Global Financial Crisis of 2008–2009, which arguably could have been averted by tighter regulation of the US banking sector, has been estimated at $11.9 trillion by the International Monetary Fund (IMF), or, in plain terms, one-fifth of annual global world output (Daily Telegraph, 2009). The impact of this US crisis has had an international impact, while also being felt by the wider society, with millions of Americans being in danger of losing their homes, metropolitan areas experiencing higher unemployment rates, and many households experiencing a decline in net wealth combined with reduced access to credit. This impact on wider society has also been felt outside the US, with some households in the UK also experiencing a decline in net wealth as a consequence of low interest rates or reduced access to credit.

When examining the impact on UK banking, the forecast losses at HBOS of 'nearly 11 billion' (British Broadcasting Corporation, 2009) that necessitated state intervention also fall well below the latest estimated private sector losses to fraud, which total £21.2 billion (NFA, 2013, p. 17). The financial and insurance sector contribute £5.4 billion to this (NFA, 2013, p. 17), which includes an estimate of £1 billion for mortgage fraud, this figure being only £0.2 billion lower than the estimated losses for benefit fraud (NFA, 2013, p. 34), which receives significantly more government attention. Estimated mortgage lending during 2012 totalled £143 billion (NFA, 2013, p. 42), and when applying the average loss figure to fraud of 5.7 per cent and the highest percentage loss figure of 10.6 per cent (Button and Gee, 2013, p. 16), the true extent of mortgage fraud losses could range between £8 billion and £15 billion. When taking account of the continued pressure applied by the state to increase lending, it is conceivable that these losses could be even higher, thus

DOI: 10.1057/9781137406286.0006

emphasizing the need to adopt a more accurate measure, which current indications suggest that the financial institutions are reluctant to implement voluntarily.

Data on the private sector reveals that the total turnover across all business sizes is £3.1 trillion (NFA, 2013, p. 17). Similarly, when applying the average loss to fraud figure of 5.7 per cent (Button and Gee, 2013, p. 73) to this figure, losses could be as high as £0.18 trillion, which far exceeds the estimate of £21.2 billion for the whole of the UK private sector (NFA, 2013, p. 17). These potential private sector losses to fraud certainly warrant consideration of state intervention into other industries apart from the financial services sector; specifically those experiencing large scale losses, including wholesale and retail trade, repair of motor vehicles and motorcycles, manufacturing, mining, utilities, information and communication, waste management and transportation (NFA, 2012, p. 18).

It is also worth examining perception surveys of UK private sector businesses conducted by the NFA during 2011 and 2012. The first survey took the form of a snowball sample using contacts within the private sector and resulted in 202 respondents completing the questionnaire (NFA, 2012, p. 16). What is of concern is that no information is supplied by the NFA regarding the response rate. Of equal concern is that only '79.2% of respondents said they agree or strongly agree that their organization is at risk from fraud' (NFA, 2012, p. 16). Respondents were also asked to provide an estimate of fraud against their organization as a percentage of annual turnover, however 'almost half of respondents chose the option "prefer not to say"' (NFA, 2012, p. 16). While this information may be commercially sensitive, it suggests a reluctance to supply estimated fraud loss data to the NFA, let alone accurate data. This reluctance to supply such an estimate might be because the organization has no idea whatsoever of the extent of their fraud losses which gives even more cause for concern.

Of further interest are the findings from the NFA's 2012 qualitative survey undertaken with 45 private sector organizations participating in the quantitative survey 'to understand better the considerations for estimating fraud loss'. The significant responses being that many organizations 'felt that it was too difficult to place a precise figure on an activity they did not know about' and that they 'may have more hidden fraud occurring than they had originally considered' (NFA, 2013, p. 20). These issues can be addressed by the creation of a British Standard of fraud measurement, supported by the creation of an information exchange matrix to improve understanding of the fraud loss measurement process.

The issue of cost is also relevant when advocating mandating the measurement of fraud, with a potential argument to be countered being that conducting fraud loss measurement exercises is too expensive to be financially viable. Historically this may have been the case, with one exercise taking 'six people six months to complete' (Button and Gee, 2013, p. 76). However, 'advances in technology and process have reduced this to 100–150 days and progress will see these figures reduce further in coming years' (Button and Gee, 2013, p. 76). The costs are not excessive and once organizations are made aware of this, the probability of compliance may increase. A further argument proffered when advocating the benefits of fraud loss measurement is profitability. For example, applying the global average loss rate of 5.7 per cent to the 255 companies in the FTSE (Financial Times and Stock Exchange) 350 who posted financial returns and were profitable, the average increase in profitability 'would be almost 36 per cent' (Button and Gee, 2013, p. 187). Accordingly, this statistic offers additional persuasion of the potential organizational benefits of the proposed options for change.

Case studies from both the UK and US where adopting this process has resulted in financial benefits offer empirical evidence that fraud loss measurement is cost effective. These include:

▸ The NHS, which had a budget of £87.2 billion for 2005/2006, reduced losses by up to 60 per cent during the period 1998 and 2006, and by up to 40 per cent over a shorter period (National Health Service Counter Fraud and Security Management Service, 2007).

▸ The US Department of Agriculture reduced losses by 28 per cent within a £12 billion dollar program between 2002 and 2004 (United States Department of Agriculture, 2002, 2003, 2004).

▸ The Department for Work and Pensions reduced losses in the two means tested benefits Income Support and Jobseekers Allowance that have an annual expenditure of £11.4 billion by 50 per cent between 1997/1998 and 2005/2006 (Department for Work and Pensions, 2007).

The US provides another example of regulatory intervention aimed at addressing the risks posed by fraudulent activity, in the form of the Sarbanes–Oxley Act 2002 (SOX). The financial impact of the respective collapses of Enron and WorldCom, particularly the former company who filed what was then the largest bankruptcy in US history, was felt globally, but significantly in the US. As a consequence of public outcry, President George W. Bush tasked Senator Paul Sarbanes and Congressman Mike Oxley to create legislation that would avert any repeat of corporate scandals such as Enron and WorldCom. The ensuing statute created the most radical set of financial auditing changes in the US since the 1930s (Moeller, 2004, p. 3; Murphy and Topyan, 2005). The resultant expansion of federal regulation was aimed at making all corporate financial accounting and reporting more reliable (Ambler, Massaro and Acre, 2010, p. 3). One significant component of this regulation, and of particular relevance to the proposals of this book, is the Act's imposition of corporate certification requirements, whereby chief executives and chief financial officers are required to certify the Company's published statements. This process of self-certification and developing best practice offers a model to inform the proposals made by this research.

This statute has achieved some impact on addressing fraud risk and the resultant public harm, through the introduction of the requirement for management reporting of internal control (Gupta and Leech, 2006, p. 39); increasing penalties for financial statement fraud (Tackett, Woolf and Claypole, 2004, p. 349); prohibition of auditing consulting services structuring transactions (Cullinan, 2004, p. 861) and providing middle management with a reason to resist pressure 'to be creative with their numbers' (Wyant, 2003, p. 578). The importance of this legislation has been acknowledged internationally, with 'the rest of the world' considering enacting 'SOX like legislation' (Gupta and Leech, 2006, p. 450). Of further significance is the fact that the provisions of the act have global impact, with overseas companies that have securities registered or listed in the US having to comply with the Act's requirements. (Cardilli, 2003, p. 790; Litvak, 2006, p. 11). A similar provision is worthy of consideration within any proposed UK statute mandating the measurement of fraud.

The Bribery Act 2010 provides another example of state intervention into the private sector. Section 7 of this statute creates an offence which may be committed by a commercial organization should they fail to prevent persons who perform services for or on behalf of that organization from bribing another on their behalf, and are unable to evidence that they had the necessary safeguards in place to prevent such activity taking place. So if the Government intervenes in such a manner for bribery, by laying down mandatory obligations to private sector organizations to

DOI: 10.1057/9781137406286.0006

implement specified processes at a cost to the business, why not impose similar mandatory requirements for the measurement of fraud, which will actually benefit the organization?

Additionally, Section 9 of the Bribery Act stipulates that the Secretary of State must publish guidance on procedures that will assist organizations to comply with the legislation. This has been issued, including a '*Quick Start Guide*' (Ministry of Justice, 2011) which performs the function of a manual of guidance. Furthermore, and of relevance to the research argument, this legislation is supported by a British Standard 10500 which provides an anti-bribery management system for organizations and is applicable to all organizations in the public, private and voluntary/charitable sectors. This system introduces a significant number of measures resulting in costs to the organizations, including 'the adoption and communication of an anti-bribery policy, training and guidance for employees, appointing a compliance manager, undertaking risk assessment and due diligence, controlling gifts and hospitality, implementing effective procurement, commercial and financial controls, and instituting reporting and investigation procedures' (British Standards Institute Case Study, n.d.).

Finally, this book offers the observations of the United States General Accounting Office (2001) who argue that the biggest obstacle to the management of improper payments is the culture of denial within organizations. This research therefore argues that to develop accurate fraud loss measurement three valid and co-ordinated options for change have been identified.

Review

This chapter has outlined the proposed options for change to support the development of a more accurate fraud measure. Justification for state intervention mandating such measurement has also been argued, this being evidenced by the government's intervention during the banking crisis and the regulatory requirements imposed by the Bribery Act 2010. Further evidence from the US in support of this argument has been presented in the form of the SOX which imposes federal regulation prescribing internal accounting and auditing processes on private sector organizations.

DOI: 10.1057/9781137406286.0006

3

The Dark Figure of Fraud

Abstract: *The term dark figure is used to describe the difference between what is the actual level of crime and that which appears in statistics. This chapter introduces the concept of the dark figure of fraud which results from the limited attention fraud receives within crime statistics and surveys. The focus then moves to a thematic review of extant fraud loss measurement data outputs, paying particular attention to accuracy, reliability and comparability. It also considers methodologies and issues identified in existing literature on the measurement of fraud.*

Tunley, Martin. *Mandating the Measurement of Fraud: Legislating against Loss.* Basingstoke, Palgrave Macmillan, 2014. DOI: 10.1057/9781137406286.0007.

DOI: 10.1057/9781137406286.0007

The dark figure of fraud

Many frauds remain undiscovered, and therefore absent from official returns. Consequently, police recorded statistics, and data compiled by agencies such as the Department for Work and Pensions (DWP) only capture a limited amount of fraud (Doig and Levi, 2009; Doig and Macaulay, 2010; Gannon and Doig, 2010), thus contributing to what may be described as the dark figure of fraud. The earliest acknowledgement of the possible existence of a dark figure of fraud may in fact come from Sutherland (1940), who identifies a lack of recognition of white collar crime in police-recorded statistics. White collar crime being defined as 'crimes committed by persons of respectability and high social status in the course of their occupations' (Sutherland and Cressey, 1960, p. 40). Sutherland (1940) concludes that this is because prosecution is frequently avoided due to the status of the parties involved, that the offences are often considered trivial, and on occasions it is difficult to gather sufficient evidence. This explanation is still valid in terms of the underrepresentation of fraud within official crime statistics due to the fact that only a small proportion of frauds are recorded by the criminal justice system (Allen et al., 2005). The dark figure of fraud may actually result from the fact that 'many frauds are not seen by individual victims as crimes that warrant reporting to the authorities', or alternatively, 'the hassle, or culpable embarrassment of informing the authorities may outweigh the desire to report the scam' (Sutton, 2007, p. 250).

Following the refinement of criminal statistics, more types of 'private criminality' have been studied, such as white collar crime, yet they still remain significantly underrepresented within recorded crime statistics (Maguire, 2007, p. 247). A potential explanation is that 'the relationship between frequency and seriousness is not straightforward'. Consequently, 'fraud and forgery appear in recorded crime figures in relatively small numbers'; however if the measure focused on value stolen, 'fraud would come out as of greater significance than other categories with many times the number of recorded offences' (Maguire, 2007, p. 265). To address this issue, the criteria for crime statistical recording should incorporate monetary value in addition to frequency, and through an awareness campaign, individual victims encouraged to report losses.

DOI: 10.1057/9781137406286.0007

Fraud within crime statistics

The main source of fraud data within crime statistics is provided by the police. Police-recorded crime data 'provides a count of fraud, based on legal definitions and according to National Crime Recording Standards and Home Office Counting Rules'; however they are 'generally considered to be a poor indication of the real level and trends' (Hoare, 2007, p. 265). This limited representation results from the fact that fraud and forgery offences are particularly susceptible to underreporting (Allen et al., 2005, p. 1; Coleman and Moynihan, 1996, p. 8), often because victims are unaware of the fraud, or elect not to report the incident to the police (Fraud Review Team, 2006, p. 7). Accordingly, this offence may not find its way into either the official crime statistics or victim surveys, thus contributing to the dark figure of fraud.

One exception is card fraud data produced by the Home Office which uses data supplied by UK Payments because this fraud typology is often reported directly to the card issuer rather than the police (Nicholas, Kershaw and Walker, 2007, p. 86). These data are now incorporated into the *Crime in England and Wales* report (Office for National Statistics, 2012). The principal explanation for this level of reliability is that the credit card fraud is likely to be reported because the consumer no longer bears any financial liability once reported to the card issuer. The crime statistics produced by the Office of National Statistics include fraud data from the National Fraud Intelligence Bureau (Office for National Statistics, 2012), which assist in providing a slightly more realistic picture of fraud offences numerically.

Following the introduction of the Fraud Act 2006, the way in which the police record crime has changed due to the introduction of an economic crime category (Maguire, 2012, p. 213). This is encouraging because it raises the profile of fraud within official crime statistics; however changes in this recording process means that 'year on year comparisons are only possible from 2007/2008 onwards' (Office of National Statistics, 2012, p. 60). A further development which may also assist in reducing the dark figure results from the National Statistician's review of Crime Statistics in England and Wales (National Statistician, 2011), which identifies fraud as a significant gap within these statistics, and that data should be provided from additional sources. At the time of writing, one positive development is the recent announcement that to centralize the fraud reporting process and the recording of statistical data, the national fraud and cyber

DOI: 10.1057/9781137406286.0007

crime reporting centre (Action Fraud) will become part of the City of London Police from April 2014.

Fraud in crime surveys

The British Crime Survey (BCS) 'is used to examine new or emerging types of crime such as fraud' (Jansson, 2007, p. 30). However, it only covers debit and credit card fraud, identity fraud and mass marketing fraud. Furthermore, a significant difficulty in using crime surveys to measure fraud is that there is often a delay between the fraud and its actual discovery. Equally, 'evolving crimes, such as Internet fraud can be difficult to keep up with on a large scale continuous survey' (Hoare, 2007, pp. 267–268). This criticism is particularly relevant to the measurement of fraud, because evidence suggests that fraudsters are frequently turning to cyber crime because the Internet offers a quick and effective medium for their scams (Thomas and Loader, 2003). Consequently, to be of value, it is imperative that the BCS keeps up to date with new and emerging crimes, such as cybercrime.

A further omission within the BCS is that it excludes fraud against businesses. Nevertheless, there have been some surveys conducted by private sector organizations (British Retail Consortium, 2009; Price-WaterhouseCoopers, 2011) that have attempted to measure fraud by surveying a random selection of businesses. Unfortunately these surveys are somewhat unreliable due to their small or unrepresentative sample, and lack of consistency in methodologies.

There have also been some government-led victimization and offender surveys incorporating fraud offences within the data-gathering process, thus making some progress in illuminating the dark figure of fraud. The 2003 Offending, Crime and Justice Survey (Budd, Sharp and Mayhew, 2005) includes fraud, and was the first offender survey to incorporate this crime typology. The survey includes benefit fraud, tax fraud credit and debit card fraud and insurance fraud. The findings of this survey are combined with supplementary modules in the 2002/2003 BCS which asks respondents about fraud and technology crimes, which are presented as a thematic report (Allen et al., 2005). The exercise was repeated in the 2004/2005 BCS and an updated report issued (Wilson, Patterson, Powell and Hembury, 2006).

The first *Commercial Victimization Survey*, which includes fraud against businesses, was conducted in 1994 (Mirrlees-Black and Ross,

DOI: 10.1057/9781137406286.0007

1995); however the follow-up was not conducted until 2002 (Shury, Speed, Vivian, Kuechel and Nicholas, 2005). The most recent survey at the time of writing was conducted in 2012 (Home Office, 2013). Surveys of this nature and the aforementioned report on fraud and technology crimes do offer some useful information, but have minimal impact in terms of eradicating the dark figure of fraud simply, because they are not produced on a regular enough basis and require an increased sample size. Furthermore, within the commercial victimization survey, the questions concerning fraud are located among those relating to higher impact crime typologies, and thus may be overlooked. To develop a more informed picture of the extent and nature of fraud, these surveys should be conducted more frequently and be fraud-specific.

To make inroads into reducing the dark figure of fraud, there is a need to increase awareness of fraud as a crime, with more emphasis placed on the importance of reporting fraud, and in the case of organizations, a 'memorandum of understanding' issued by the police that may help 'clarify any dilemmas directors have' about reporting fraud (Higson, 1999, p. 2). These proposals will actually contribute to a more accurate picture of fraud within official crime and survey data, because improved awareness should result in increased reporting, or more answers in the affirmative when being surveyed, and hopefully, an increase in organizations conducting fraud loss measurement exercises.

Identified methodologies and issues

Having reviewed fraud measurement methodologies, the first two worthy of discussion are bottom up and top down (Levi et al., 2007, p. 19; Levi and Burrows, 2008, p. 306). The former is used to calculate the costs of fraud from an organizational perspective, whereas a top-down methodology estimates fraud from a national perspective (Levi and Burrows, 2008, p. 306). An example of the former is where an annual loss figure is merely the sum of all reported frauds. A 'top-down' macro approach involves the creation of an estimated figure using linked datasets, possibly sourced externally, which consequently renders it more exposed to error, and limitations in statistical certainty than a bottom-up approach.

Gee, Button and Brooks (2009, p. 7) identify two typologies of fraud measurement: a percentage loss rate (PLR) and a fraud frequency rate (FFR). The PLR shows the proportion of expenditure lost to fraud and error, whereas a FFR details the frequency of fraud and error. The authors correctly point out that the same exercise can produce different PLR and FFR figures, dependent upon the value of fraudulent items of expenditure.

Another fraud measurement methodology with limitations calculates losses based on successfully detected cases. Gee (2010b) rightly observes that 'no unlawful act has a 100% detection rate and the essence of fraud is deception and concealment' (p. 24). Interestingly, organizations conducting measurement exercises using common sampling have identified that detection rates rarely exceed 1 in 30 (Gee, 2010b, p. 24), which offers additional evidence to suggest that this approach to measurement is flawed. What gives further cause for concern, and further evidences the need for a sea change in the approach to measurement, is the fact that the Cabinet Office's Fraud, Error and Debt (FED) Taskforce (Her Majesty's Government, 2012), while seeking a reduction in the impact of fraud and error, are still advocating the use of this methodology, rather than compelling central government departments to undertake proactive measurement exercises.

Obstacles to accurate measurement

> Levels of Fraud are extremely difficult to quantify.
> (National Fraud Strategic Authority, 2008, p. 1)

The Fraud Review Team (2006, p. 23) identify two problems when measuring fraud, these being:

▸ having clear definitions of what constitutes fraud,
▸ having robust and transparent mechanisms for measuring fraud.

Underreporting often results from a reluctance to accept fraud losses as a legitimate business cost and is considered a significant barrier to accurate fraud measurement (Foresight Crime Prevention Panel, 2006, p. 10). Maxfield, Hough and Mayhew (2007, p. 306) suggest that companies may be resistant to revealing much about the presence of fraud. As a consequence, fraud statistics 'should be viewed as the lowest reliable figure, rather than a true full-blown picture' (Jones and Levi, 2000, p. 9).

Russell (1998, pp. 5–6) reports survey findings that reveal 'only a fifth of finance directors ... would report an incident of suspected fraud' (p. 5), because of a 'concern that it would become public knowledge'. Blunt and

DOI: 10.1057/9781137406286.0007

Hand (2007, p. 24) suggest that companies are reticent to report fraud because they are concerned about:

▶ length and cost of legal proceedings
▶ risk to the company's reputation
▶ hazy definitions of fraud
▶ belief that authorities place a low priority on fraud
▶ the easiest option may be to dismiss the individual concerned.

This reluctance by companies to report crime is not specific to fraud; however, as evidenced by the *2012 Commercial Victimization Survey* which reveals low reporting rates on many crimes including assaults, theft by persons unknown and thefts by employees (Home Office, 2013, p. 21). To achieve a more accurate picture of private sector fraud, mandating measurement may be an option worth considering, this being supported by an awareness campaign on the associated business benefits. This in turn may result in companies becoming more willing not just to measure but also to report fraud, thus providing a more accurate representation of private sector fraud in UK loss data and official crime statistics.

One problem to overcome is that there are numerous grey areas. For example, two activities that might be committed with fraudulent intent but may also go undetected are

▶ Default on personal loans or credit cards where the borrower had no intention of repaying.
▶ Bankruptcy or Individual Voluntary Arrangements used as a means of avoiding debts.

(Blunt and Hand, 2007, p. 23)

To remove this grey area, the above should be considered within a common sample during any measurement exercise and incorporated into loss data.

The perceived excessive cost of conducting fraud loss measurement exercises also impacts on the accuracy of any overall picture being developed. Simply because many organizations believe these costs to be prohibitive, and fail to recognize the benefits of regularly measuring fraud losses.

The costs of measurement exercises are dependent upon:

▶ The frequency of the estimating exercise.
▶ The sample sizes checked.

▶ The work involved in checking each case sampled.
▶ The work involved in validating the results.
(National Audit Office, 2008a, p. 15)

Despite such cost implications, the advantage of regular measurement exercises is actually acknowledged by the National Audit Office (2008b, p. 15) who argue that they enable a department to 'track changes over time in the estimated fraud loss', thus enabling organizations to evaluate the effectiveness of reduction strategies.

This chapter now reviews and develops a taxonomy of fraud data outputs.

Statistically valid loss measurement surveys

This review initially examines fraud data outputs considered to use robust loss measurement methodologies. The selection criteria have been informed by critical evaluation of methodology, specifically, data sources, sampling methodologies and levels of statistical confidence.

Department for Work and Pensions

The DWP 'began a continuous rolling measurement of Income Support and Jobseekers Allowance in 1997, recognising their vulnerability to fraud loss' (Hoare, 2007, p. 269). When examining data quality, the Benefit Fraud Inspectorate (1998, p. 19) conclude that there are 'a number of weaknesses in the way fraud is measured'. When comparing the measurement methodology, it is worth noting that DWP rely upon a criminal-based evidential test informed by the conditions of benefit entitlement, thus placing emphasis on beyond reasonable doubt.

Some of these historical shortcomings in data quality have been addressed, and more statistically robust estimates of losses are the outcome. For example, *Fraud and Error in the Benefits System: April 2007 to March 2008* (DWP, 2008, p. 2) provides estimates for the means tested benefits Income Support, Jobseekers Allowance, Pension Credit and Housing Benefit, based on 'analysis of random samples drawn from the benefit caseloads'. These data presented are subject to some 'statistical uncertainty', which is quantified in the form of '95% confidence intervals'. A lack of statistical robustness of certain measures is acknowledged, for example, assumptions being made about benefits which have not been

DOI: 10.1057/9781137406286.0007

reviewed on a regular basis. This trend has continued with extant data being subject to 'statistical sampling uncertainties' and that 'a proportion of continuously measured benefit expenditure cannot be captured by the sampling process' (DWP, 2013, p. 11).

One recurring shortcoming of benefit fraud data is the fact that DWP only measure on a continuous basis those benefits accounting for 25 per cent of total expenditure (DWP, 2013, p. 8). 'Occasional reviews' are conducted on benefits that account for 59 per cent of total expenditure and the remaining benefits accounting for 16 per cent of total expenditure go 'unreviewed' (DWP, 2013, p. 10). When considering that these unreviewed benefits actually account for expenditure in 2012/2013 of £26 billion (DWP, 2013, p. 15), this further suggests that there is further work required to establish a more accurate picture of benefit fraud.

Even taking into account these limitations, through the use of continuous rolling measurement exercises, DWP data are far more statistically reliable than any other government department, with the exception of historical NHS data.

National Health Service

The task of measuring healthcare fraud is challenging, with offences being committed by patients, pharmacists, dentists, opticians, doctors, hospital consultants and staff (National Health Service, 1999, pp. 34–37). This requires a significant commitment in terms of measurement exercises, and because of the volume and diverse nature of fraud, the decision to measure each area of spend separately is well-judged.

Within each individual measurement exercise, the NHS Counter Fraud Service (NHSCFS) validates data on a case-by-case basis, decisions being made using a civil definition of fraud. On the one hand, this may be considered a tactical decision because the civil burden of proof is based on the balance of probabilities, and thus any measurement exercise may appear to uncover more fraud than by applying the test of 'beyond reasonable doubt'. On the other hand, because the NHS are required to measure such a wide range of estimated fraud the decision to adopt a universal definition is sound judgement.

To further progress the measurement strategy, *Countering Fraud in the NHS* identifies the need to 'develop a robust measure of the amount of fraud that exists' to accurately target 'available resources at areas most at risk' (National Health Service, 1999, p. 10). Concentrating upon one area of fraud (prescription fraud) allowed the NHS to pilot test the measurement processes and develop best practice before rolling out to other high risk areas.

Countering Fraud in the NHS: Identifying the nature and scale of the problem unveils the Risk Measurement Project (RMP) which measures fraud using 'statistically valid samples of cases in each area of NHS spending' (National Health Service Counter Fraud and Security Management Service, 2001a, p. 2). Most importantly, this strategy acknowledges that 'information about the money that is lost to fraud' may be used to illustrate 'where savings have been made', which may then 'inform the development of preventative measures' (National Health Service Counter Fraud and Security Management Service, 2001a, pp. 2–3). This approach of publicly acknowledging the value of fraud loss data is sadly lacking within other government departments.

An improvement in the accuracy of fraud loss data through the use of common sampling (NHS Counter Fraud and Security Management Service, 2001b, p. 31) has enabled effective targeting of the counter-fraud tactical resource (Gee, 2010b, p. 25). One concern however is that having made progress in developing measurement strategies, the NHS have not published any loss figures since 2006 (Gee, 2010b, p. 25; Philips, 2010). The only NHS-specific data contained within the *Annual Fraud Indicator* (NFA, 2013) is that of patient charges fraud. Any other NHS-specific fraud appears to have been absorbed into the remaining fraud by typology data, which therefore offers a less accurate picture of healthcare fraud than available prior to the NFA collating fraud loss data. With the future of the Annual Fraud Indicator being in doubt due to the closure of the NFA it is possible we may see a return to more detailed fraud loss data outputs from this department.

Measuring detected fraud

This book now examines reports utilizing data from successful investigations, where fraud has been proven based on the evidential test applied by each organization. There are additional reports that incorporate detected fraud, but have been allocated an alternative classification within this review. Paradoxically, the only report falling within this section that relies wholly on detected cases is published by the Audit Commission.

DOI: 10.1057/9781137406286.0007

Audit Commission

The Audit Commission's (2010) report *Protecting the Public Purse 2010* contains the results from the survey of detected fraud committed against councils. In contrast to previous surveys, the Audit Commission 'made submission of 2009/2010 survey data mandatory', of significance however is the statistic that a return rate of 94 per cent was achieved (Audit Commission, 2010, p. 10). The response rate for the subsequent report improved to 99 per cent (Audit Commission, 2011) and has now improved to 100 per cent (Audit Commission, 2013, p. 10). The fact that it has taken the Audit Commission some time to actually achieve total compliance suggests that a statute that mandates fraud measurement but also contains sufficient penalties for non-compliance may be a better option.

One interesting observation is that despite the Audit Commission offering a definition of fraud (p. 10), 'some councils do not record all types of fraud, or do not always classify all fraudulent activity as fraud' (Audit Commission, 2010, p. 11). There has been some improvement, with public bodies 'classifying more incidents correctly as fraud' (Audit Commission, 2011, p. 7).

Nevertheless, if fraud is to be measured accurately, there is need for both a recognized definition of fraud and standard of accuracy that are applied when conducting mandatory loss measurement exercises. In conclusion, these documents are useful for comparing the levels of fraud investigation activity by individual local authorities. However, they fail to offer a full and accurate picture of local government fraud losses, and may continue to do so until all local authorities are compelled to correctly record all frauds.

Guestimates

This section examines fraud loss publications containing data that are considered little more than guestimates. For the purpose of this review, documents falling within this criterion contain data collected using a flawed collection plan or possess significant caveats on reliability, or limited disclosure of methodology. This segment is mainly populated by reports produced by private sector organizations advertising their accounting and auditing capability, rather than collecting meaningful fraud loss data. This discussion will however commence with the public sector documents which worryingly fall into the guestimate category

DOI: 10.1057/9781137406286.0007

despite the cabinet office strategy to improve the quality and accuracy of public sector fraud loss data.

British Broadcasting Corporation

The British Broadcasting Corporation (BBC) match their data with the Office of the Deputy Prime Minister's count of the number of homes, which is then matched against 'TV penetration data' supplied by the Broadcasters Audience Research Board (Fraud Review Team, 2006, p. 328). The evasion rate totalling £195 million is estimated at 5.3 per cent 'which is a calculation of the number of premises where no licence is held but a licence is believed to be needed' (TV Licensing, 2009, p. 8). The overall loss figure is very subjective, being reliant upon the accuracy of third party data, and no account is taken of whether these dwellings are occupied. Consequently the confidence level should be rated as low and the resultant data considered nothing more than guestimates.

Driver and Vehicle Licensing Agency

'Estimates of Vehicle Excise Duty (VED) evasion are derived from periodic roadside surveys' (Fraud Review Team, 2006, p. 329). The evasion rate is calculated using Department for Transport vehicle sightings data collected annually during June from 250 locations. These data are then compared with the licensing status record of each vehicle, enabling a national estimate of VED lost through evasion (Driver and Vehicle Licensing Agency [DVLA], 2009, p. 51). VED evasion is calculated at £50m, which equates to less than 1 per cent of total due (DVLA, 2009, p. 9). This fails to stand up to scrutiny; first, because the sample is limited in terms of representation, and secondly, the figure of 1 per cent falls significantly below the average public sector loss of 4.57 per cent (Gee, Button and Brooks, 2010, p. 4). VED evasion data harvested using the same methodology is now incorporated into the *Annual Fraud Indicator*, and for 2011/2012 was estimated to be £40 million, this being 0.7 per cent of revenue (NFA, 2013, p. 56), which when compared with the aforementioned average public sector loss, again raises questions on the accuracy of these data.

Foreign and Commonwealth Office

The Foreign and Commonwealth Office (FCO) investigates fraud relating to operational procedures (FCO, 2010); however no specific information is provided on what fraud typologies are considered. When

DOI: 10.1057/9781137406286.0007

attempting to measure fraud, the Department's main predicament is that data are collected from a wide geographical area and they rely upon 'data received from third parties' (Hoare, 2007, p. 270). Consequently, data are considered to have very minimal statistical confidence, the resultant loss figure being considered nothing more than a guestimate and the contribution towards constructing an accurate picture of public sector fraud losses being minimal.

Her Majesty's Treasury

Her Majesty's Treasury's (2009a) *2008–2009 Fraud Report* 'analyses data submitted by central government departments and their agencies about fraud and theft perpetrated by staff' (p. 5). The findings concentrate upon 'fraud relating to departments' administrative affairs' and exclude 'fraud perpetrated by external fraudsters' (p. 3). Disappointingly, the findings are only based on data supplied by '45 central government bodies', which reveals that 20 departments submitted a nil return (p. 5). When judging the accuracy of public sector fraud losses, this observation casts significant doubt on the reliability of these data. It is no surprise therefore that the report includes the caveat that it is 'not a definitive account of all frauds affecting government departments during the relevant period' (p. 5). What is uncertain is whether these departments have conducted measurement exercises and found no evidence of fraud, failed to detect fraud or simply not bothered measuring and just sent a nil return.

The lack of suggestion within the report that questions have been raised concerning these missing data proffers further evidence to support the argument for mandating public sector fraud measurement. Furthermore, it is of concern that external fraud is not measured, nor any explanation offered concerning its omission. Of equal interest is the fact that this document is no longer produced, it being considered to have 'served its purpose', and that the Treasury should withdraw, 'as the National Fraud Authority begins to build and share knowledge in central government' (Her Majesty's Treasury, 2009b). Since April 2011 all central government departments have been required to complete a quarterly data summary which includes data on fraud, error and debt which are published by HM Treasury (NFA, 2013, p. 15). However, there continues to be evidence of nil returns for fraud, and some data summaries fail to mention fraud. Furthermore, it is difficult to verify how these returns are policed and consequently whether fraud has been measured and found

DOI: 10.1057/9781137406286.0007

not to be present or whether departments are submitting a nil return unchallenged.

Her Majesty's Revenue and Customs

Her Majesty's Revenue and Customs (HMRC) employ different methodologies to measure fraud because they have a large number of inputs and outputs to measure. This review commences by exploring the measurement of taxation losses.

To measure indirect taxation, actual tax receipts are compared against a potential yield informed by external statistics on consumption. Regrettably, these estimates include generous confidence intervals because consumption estimates are uncertain. In contrast, because there is no reliable equivalent source for direct taxation, 'it is difficult to establish ... the value ... of this type of fraud' (Hoare, 2007, p. 269).

The introduction to *Measuring Indirect Tax Losses-2007* advises that 'estimating the scale of ... revenue losses is not only inherently difficult, but also a relatively untested area of work for governments in the EU' (HMRC, 2007, p. 3). Within the updated document *Measuring Tax Gaps-2009*, HMRC (2009, p. 4) reveal that they have 'developed estimates for tax gaps for the main direct and indirect taxes that are the best possible based on the available information'. A 'top-down approach' is used to measure indirect taxes, whereby the tax gap is estimated by subtracting tax paid from an estimate of revenue due. Due to the uncertainty of the estimates however, methodologies are regularly reviewed.

The methodology for measuring Value Added Tax (VAT) losses compares 'the net theoretical tax liabilities with actual VAT receipts, the difference between these amounts being known as the VAT gap' (HMRC, 2009, p. 39), which disappointingly is also 'subject to a degree of uncertainty' (p. 36). Consequently, HMRC (2009) advise that they are unable to produce a precise confidence interval in respect of VAT loss estimates (p. 36).

When discussing Missing Trader Intra-Community VAT fraud (carousel fraud), HMRC (2009) are vague in describing their measurement methodology, but do reveal that a 'bottom-up approach' is applied 'to estimate attempted fraud and its impact on VAT receipts' (p. 12). Excise gaps also include spirits, cigarettes and hand-rolling tobacco, being defined as the amount of duty and VAT not collected due to illicit purchases. Losses are measured using a top-down technique, calculating

DOI: 10.1057/9781137406286.0007

the illicit market as total consumption minus legitimate consumption. Minimal confidence can be placed in these data, HMRC advising that 'it is not possible to provide an accurate single estimate of the illicit market for spirits and tobacco' (p. 14).

A further limitation relates to estimated losses for cigarettes, calculated using General Household Survey data which only becomes available 12 months after completion of the survey (HMRC, 2007, p. 16). Estimates of losses are therefore always behind loss data for other commodities, which limits any meaningful aggregated analysis of fraud loss data. All figures presented 'are subject to statistical uncertainty caused by sampling and systematic errors in the data, resulting in estimates that are either too low or too high', thus generating 'margins of error within which the true value would be expected to lie 95 per cent of the time' (HMRC, 2009, p. 36).

A similar caveat is contained within the HMRC (2013a) statistical release, declaring that the data presented are subject to both random and systematic errors. This suggests that a revision of collection methodology and data sources is urgently required to facilitate more reliable loss measurement. The continuing issue is the reliance upon third party data, many of which have limited confidence levels, which may skew HMRC fraud loss data. Arguably, this lack of a robust data collection methodology by such an important public sector department further evidences a pressing requirement to mandate fraud measurement to a prescribed level of accuracy.

Child and Working Tax Credits presents the results from the first random enquiry program measuring tax credit fraud and error (HMRC, 2006, p. 2). A random stratified sample of 4,500 cases is reviewed, the results being 'scaled up ... to estimate the overall level of error and fraud in the tax credit system' (p. 2). Fraud levels are calculated to a 95 per cent confidence level (p. 3), but subject to 'sampling errors' (p. 8), which cast doubt upon data accuracy. Furthermore, the rigour may also be questioned because not all cases in the original sample were used (p. 9). Lamentably, a review of extant data output (HMRC, 2013b) indicates that despite a developing awareness of the limitations of fraud loss data, no progress has been made to improve the robustness of these data.

Ministry of Defence

> 'Right back to the time of Samuel Pepys and before, the task of supplying and supporting military forces has attracted thieves and fraudsters'
>
> (Ministry of Defence [MOD], 2011, p. 1)

DOI: 10.1057/9781137406286.0007

The MOD 'Defence Fraud Analysis Unit' (DFAU) 'provides estimates based on reports from line managers or whistleblowers' (Hoare, 2007, p. 266). There is limited clarity in the data offered, and it is difficult to establish exactly how many of the cases reported on actually involve fraud as opposed to theft. Accordingly, these data should be attributed a low confidence level, and considered nothing more than a guestimate.

This chapter now reviews the private sector data outputs categorized as guestimates within this taxonomy.

Association of British Insurers

The Association of British Insurers (ABI, 2009, p. 1) research brief *General Insurance Claims Fraud* estimates that undetected general insurance claims fraud 'total £1.9 billion a year'. In estimating the cost of undetected fraud, the ABI employ an amalgam of data collection techniques including:

- Interviews with:
  - ten insurers accounting for over half the retail and commercial general insurance markets
  - other bodies (including IFB, CIFAS and MIB) who have relevant knowledge in this area
  - several of the major loss adjustors.
- A survey of customers – as part of the ABI's Savings and Protection quarterly survey – asking about attitudes and behaviours in respect of general insurance fraud.
- A review of the relevant literature, including that relating to the relationship between crime and the economy (and by implication the likely impact of the recession).'

(ABI, 2009, p. 2)

This data collection plan is more comprehensive than those applied by most other organizations in the public and private sectors, estimates being obtained of overall fraud risk during interviews with insurers. This is a good starting point, but unfortunately, much of it is based on qualitative surveys. The quantitative data however do come with some statistical confidence which is sadly lacking within most private sector-produced reports.

UK Payments (Formerly Association for Payment Clearing Services)

Fraud the Facts, which contains payment industry fraud loss data, is published twice yearly (Association for Payment Clearing Services

DOI: 10.1057/9781137406286.0007

[APACS], 2009, p. 2). This area of fraud measurement is relatively unique, because there is a high probability that victims report fraud, simply because most account holders are likely to identify erroneous transactions on their statements. Blunt and Hand (2007, p. 9) describe these data as 'comprehensive', a view shared by the Financial Services Authority (2003, p. 14), who conclude that these 'statistics are comprehensive'. However, it is difficult to assess the reliability and validity of these data due to the source not being disclosed, the sampling methods unexplained, and no detail of how the figures have been calculated being offered. These are repeated in the 2013 edition of this report (Financial Fraud Action UK, 2013). Should these omissions be addressed, the document would offer an even more robust illustration of evidentially supportable fraud losses in this sector.

This chapter now evaluates reports categorized as hybrids, these being defined as outputs containing data from multiple sectors, commencing with one public sector publication before moving on to the private sector and concluding with the NFA's cross-sector publication.

The nature, extent and economic impact of fraud in the UK

This report 'was commissioned by the Association of Chief Police Officers and the Home Office to meet the following objectives:

▸ To determine as accurately as possible ... the nature, extent and cost of fraud to the public and private sectors.
▸ To assess critically the availability and quality of existing evidence on fraud.
▸ To recommend appropriate strategies to facilitate the comprehensive and consistent recording of data on fraud'.

(Levi et al., 2007, p. 8)

The authors suggest that to improve the quality of fraud loss data, owners of statistical systems should encourage data providers to 'expose and better estimate undiscovered fraud' (Levi et al., 2007, p. 49). However, this final recommendation may only be achieved by action that is stronger than just encouragement.

While critiquing extant fraud loss measurement methodologies and offering pertinent observations, the authors also offer their own estimate

DOI: 10.1057/9781137406286.0007

of UK fraud losses, this being £12.98 billion (Levi et al., 2007, p. 5). Paradoxically, this appears to be based on a combination of measures, all of which have weaknesses that are actually identified by the authors within their report. This suggests that there is a culture, whereby when discussing fraud losses, there is a perceived need to offer some form of loss figure, no matter how statistically robust.

National Economic Research Associates

The Economic and Social Cost of Fraud produced by National Economic Research Associates (NERA, 2000) 'provides estimates of expenditure on investigations, court proceedings and preventative measures and the amounts of money defrauded across the economy' (Brand and Price, 2000, p. 47). This is the first attempt at producing an estimate of fraud costs across all sectors, dividing it into 'discovered and undiscovered components', the former then being subdivided into reported and unreported fraud (NERA, 2000, pp. 2–3). The report also observes that reluctance by firms to report fraud may cause data collection problems, which may be rectified by using survey evidence (p. 3).

Fraud costs are divided into two types: first resource costs, which include prevention and detection costs, and secondly transfers, which are simply defined as 'the amount defrauded' (p. 4). The published data 'are based on the definitions of fraud used by those who have compiled the original statistics', consequently the figures 'may not be strictly comparable with the Home Office definition of fraud, or with each other' (NERA, 2000, p. 4). This significantly limits the value of these data for analysis, because the failure to adopt a standard definition of fraud that restricts individual interpretation renders any comparison or aggregation of data relatively meaningless.

Unsurprisingly, the report has been criticized, Doig (2006) observing there was 'no review of the methodology used' (p. 44). Furthermore, Brand and Price (2000) suspect undercounting, noting that 'the difficulty of detecting some frauds and the limited data collected...led NERA to believe that even the higher figure (of £14 billion) is likely to be an under-estimate' (p. 47). Equally, Blunt and Hand (2007) observe that NERA offer little discussion concerning 'uncertainty in measurement' (p. 11). Nevertheless, the NERA estimate of fraud was used as a baseline figure for some considerable time even though it may only be considered a guestimate.

DOI: 10.1057/9781137406286.0007

BDO

BDO's (2010) *FraudTrack 7* considers cases 'that have been through the criminal justice system and reported by the media' (p. 2); the inclusion criterion being 'cases over £50,000 from December 2008 to November 2009' (p. 30). This further illustrates that the limitations of some private sector produced fraud reports, the overall loss figure excluding a significant number of frauds because they fall under the report's 'radar'. Consequently, the figure produced underestimates the true extent of losses. The 2013 *Fraudtrack* publication continues to apply the same methodology, being based on 'all reported fraud cases over £50,000 between 01/12/2012 and 30/11/2013' (BDO, 2014).The credibility of some private sector fraud reports, often produced by auditing companies, has been challenged by Kirk (2008, p. 335) who observes that they are often designed specifically to entice corporations into using that particular organization.

KPMG Fraud Barometer

KPMG's (2010, 2012, 2014) *Fraud Barometer* examines cases relating to 'financial services, non-financial services, company, government, investors and 'other'' (Levi et al., 2007, p. 76). In terms of contributing towards an accurate picture of fraud, these data are also of limited value. The principle shortcoming being that it measures 'fraud cases in court where the loss/claim is a value over £100,000' (Fraud Review Team, 2006, p. 32), thus only capturing a portion of fraud cases. Again there is a risk of double counting data from other fraud measurement exercises supplied by the Serious Fraud Office, banks and government departments. Consequently, KPMG data offers a limited contribution in establishing an accurate representation of fraud losses from any sector.

Norwich Union

The Fraud Report (Norwich Union, 2005) was produced because no official body 'currently compiles or publishes comprehensive annual statistics on the economic cost of fraud to the UK'. The report estimates that in 2004 fraud cost the UK economy 'in the region of £16 billion' (p. 2), while also highlighting the range of wide disparities in estimates of the total cost of fraud by non-government organizations, which range from £7 to £40 billion.

DOI: 10.1057/9781137406286.0007

The methodology employed replicates the NERA (2000) survey by seeking updates from the original sources. Where extant data are unavailable, the original figures are subjected to a 12.4 per cent inflation modifier, as advised by the National Statistics Office. Conceivably, such a calculation renders these data of limited value because they fail to take account of changes in levels of fraudulent activity. Furthermore, drawing upon data supplied by various private sector organizations and the Serious Fraud Office increases the risk of double counting. Consequently, yet again the final loss figure achieved may only be considered to be a guestimate.

National Fraud Authority – Annual Fraud Indicator

The NFA's (2010a) first *Annual Fraud Indicator* aims to provide 'the best picture possible' of fraud losses, while also acknowledging that the estimate 'is some way from perfect' (p. 3). The report incorporates public and private sector data and estimates fraud losses in the charitable sector. The NFA estimate that fraud cost the UK economy £30.5 billion in 2008, but suggest this figure is a significant underestimation because certain organizations only measure reported fraud. Significantly, the report suggests that there is an urgent need for a standardized measurement of fraud, by identifying the limited value of the figures in terms of comparative analysis, because estimates from contributors utilize varying definitions and methodologies.

This report has been described as 'puzzling' by Jim Gee, former chief executive of the NHSCFS, and the figures for the health service considered 'extraordinary' (Philips, 2010). The data in dispute are the NFA figure for NHS fraud, which equates to 0.27 per cent of the budget, whereas at that time the global average had been calculated at 5.59 per cent for healthcare systems (Philips, 2010). While acknowledging these observations, this report does provide a useful starting point for developing a more accurate picture of overall fraud losses, while also illustrating there is more work required to achieve this. The principal issue being that all contributing organizations must supply data that is statistically valid by applying the same definition of fraud and standard of loss measurement.

Some concerns identified within the first report are addressed within the 2011 edition (NFA, 2011a), it being described as 'the most ... definitive assessment of fraud loss in the UK' (NFA, 2011b, p. 9). The report

DOI: 10.1057/9781137406286.0007

confirms that 'work has continued... to develop a more robust and comprehensive picture of fraud loss in the UK' (NFA, 2011a, p. 5), with fraud being estimated to cost the UK £38.4 billion a year. What has to be recognized, and this may require some education, is that increased and more accurate measurement will result in a higher loss figure. There are still data limitations however, the NFA acknowledging that 'caution must be taken when using and interpreting the figures provided, particularly when drawing comparisons between different figures' and that 'further work is still needed to improve the robustness and granularity of some of the new fraud loss estimates provided in this publication' (p. 6).

The NFA (2012) *Annual Fraud Indicator* evidences this, reporting an increased overall loss figure of £73 billion. This increase is largely attributed to changes in methodology, specifically 'direct engagement with UK businesses... to improve the comprehensiveness of loss against the private sector' (p. 6). The report suggests that this figure now includes an estimate of undetected fraud within the private sector. When examining the methodology however, the figures do not appear particularly robust. Respondents of an online survey were asked to estimate how much fraud there could be in their organization as a percentage of turn over. This estimate ranged from 3 per cent (91 respondents) to 1.4 per cent (37 respondents) (p. 16). The NFA applied the 'conservative estimate of 1.4%' to calculate private sector losses (p. 16). This falls well below both the average figure of 4.57 per cent for expenditure lost to fraud (Gee, Button and Brooks, 2009, p. 8) and the updated figure of 5.7 per cent (Button and Gee, 2013, p. 16). It is also somewhat mystifying why the NFA elected to apply this figure, thus basing the estimate for total losses within the private sector (excluding financial and insurance industries) on the opinion of 37 respondents, when a much higher proportion of respondents indicated losses at 3 per cent. What this does evidence however is that the figure for private sector losses and the overall loss figure fall well below what might actually be the true cost of fraud.

One acknowledgement contained within the 2012 report is that there are

> some limitations to the approach of using surveys to estimate areas of unknown fraud loss, such as the potential bias of organizations self-selecting to participate; the level of response rates; issues of representativeness within the samples and findings which are based on opinion rather than fact. (NFA, 2012, p. 6)

DOI: 10.1057/9781137406286.0007

This has resulted in each estimate being assigned a level of confidence ranging from excellent to poor. Interestingly, mortgage fraud has been assigned the lowest rating, and the estimated figure of £1 billion remains unchanged from the 2011 estimate. Similarly, the estimated loss for fraudulently obtained public sector assistance grants remains unchanged, the NFA observing that more work is needed to develop a more robust measurement methodology. These admissions further suggest that the overall loss figure significantly undercounts true fraud losses. Accordingly, this can only be addressed by a standard measure that would generate data with a consistent confidence level.

Moving on to examine the 2013 *Annual Fraud Indicator* (NFA, 2013), overall fraud losses are now estimated at £52 billion (p. 2). This figure comprises of identified and hidden fraud loss estimates by victim. The overall loss figure represents a reduction of £21 billion from the 2012 figure; however due to the changes in the research methodology, it is not possible to effect a year-on-year comparison. While the aim to improve accuracy of data is commendable, the fact that these changes in methodology prevents each annual figure from being used 'to trend or draw conclusions on the 'growth' or 'decline' of fraud over time' (p. 4) does render the document of limit value in terms of a holistic evaluation of the impact of counter-fraud strategies. The significant reduction in the overall loss figure, in the main, results from a decrease in private sector losses, which at £21.2 billion represents a decrease of £24.3 billion on the 2012 figure. This change is again attributable to the change in research methodology, which employed a quota sample which surveyed 500 small, medium and large businesses. What is most disappointing is the fact that these loss data are no longer presented by industry, instead being categorized by business size, with the exception of financial and insurance activities. This limits the amount of meaningful analysis of private sector fraud losses that can be undertaken using these data.

The figure of £20.6 billion for public sector losses is more convincing, representing an increase of £0.3 billion on the 2012 figure and equating to an average loss rate of 3.76 per cent. Nevertheless, some of the component data continue to be afforded confidence levels that suggest there is still room for improvement in developing a more accurate measure of fraud within this sector. For example, grant fraud data are assessed as poor, and the estimated losses to procurement fraud are only allocated an average level of confidence.

DOI: 10.1057/9781137406286.0007

This report however still fails to provide an accurate figure of overall fraud losses because of the significant gaps in, and limited reliability of, some of these data. For example, the figure of £1 million is based on the opinion of mortgage fraud experts (p. 42), rather than being measured, and remains unchanged since the initial publication of this report in 2010. These limitations are recognized by the NFA (2013), who admit that 'there are large gaps in knowledge about fraud losses' (p. 3), and as a consequence, 'the entire fraud spectrum is not captured' (p. 4).

The significant fact that the fraud loss data contained within the *Annual Fraud Indicator* 'ranges from 2006 to 2013' (NFA, 2013, p. 4) clearly indicates that in certain industries, fraud loss measurement continues to be sporadic, and arguably of low priority. I maintain this again supports the argument that it is no longer acceptable for industries to measure fraud on the ad hoc basis that the NFA appear to be content with. This is the fourth publication of this report, yet in certain calculations they continue to use data that was actually outdated when the first report was published in 2010. Additionally, the NFA (2013) identify the same limitations in the use of survey data, which were acknowledged in the 2012 report, although some attempt has been made to mitigate these through the use of increased sample sizes and 'stronger sampling strategies' (p. 5). Clearly it is time to move on from voluntary measurement and the use of perception surveys and consider some form of regulation that involves mandating measurement.

The limitations in the use of perception-based surveys rather than statistically based common sampling are clearly evidenced by the estimate from the private sector survey of 500 businesses that 'on average, fraud losses as a proportion of turnover could be in the region of 0.54 per cent' (p. 7), of which hidden losses amount to '0.36 per cent of their turnover of £2.9 trillion' (p, 18). Effecting a comparison with the research conducted by Button and Gee (2013) on statistically valid fraud loss measurement exercises that concluded that on average fraud losses amount to 5.7 per cent (p. 16) suggests this methodology is unlikely to offer anything near an accurate measure of losses for this sector. Further limitations of these private sector data are first that the estimated loss figure is actually based on the 278 respondents who 'stated that they were either 'sure' or 'very sure' in their estimate (p. 18), and secondly the 'indicative confidence interval of ±4.4 per cent on a 50 per cent finding' (p. 59), which falls significantly below the confidence level mandated within the IPIA.

The overall loss figure for financial and insurance activities also contains 'an estimate of hidden fraud losses based on assumptions'

DOI: 10.1057/9781137406286.0007

(p. 19). As a consequence, these data have been afforded a poor level of confidence by the NFA (p. 65), yet still incorporated into the report. I again maintain that this continuing use of poor quality data is unacceptable, and the only realistic option available is to mandate measurement within these two industries through regulation.

The limitations of using a perception survey are also evidenced by estimate of charity income lost to undetected fraud, which 'equates to 0.17 per cent of income' of all charities with an income of £100,000 or more (p. 23). Once again, effecting a comparison with the average fraud loss figure of 5.7 per cent (Button and Gee, 2013, p. 16) enables the conclusion to be drawn that these data may not be an accurate measure of losses. The results of the online survey of charities also suggests that there continues to be much work needed to be done to promote fraud loss measurement with only 21 per cent 'having attempted to measure their fraud loss in the last financial year' (p. 23). Furthermore, these data are only afforded a confidence level of '±2.5 per cent', and with only a 6 per cent response rate, the NFA acknowledge that 'there may be issues of representativeness and the ability to generalize' (p. 58).

In conclusion, this document offers the most accurate picture of fraud losses across all three sectors. Nonetheless, it also continues to evidence that there remains an urgent need to develop and progress improved mechanisms of measurement across all three sectors.

Impostors

This review has identified a further typology, which are classified as impostors. These publications originate from the private sector and offer no contribution to developing a more accurate picture of losses, but simply talk up fraud losses or global threats from fraudsters in an attempt to generate business. These aforementioned publications are frequently produced by auditing and accountancy companies, the first example being published by Ernst and Young, which is now discussed.

Ernst and Young

Ernst and Young's (2006) *9th Global Fraud Survey* has been included in this section because it fails to offer any specific fraud loss data. The publication actually provides the findings of a qualitative study which aims to improve understanding of how companies manage 'the risks associated with

DOI: 10.1057/9781137406286.0007

bribery of government officials outside their home countries' (p. 1). The methodology employed involves qualitative interviews with over 500 corporate leaders representing worldwide organizations (p. 3). This offers a valuable insight into the issues impacting on large global organizations, 'but is inherently limited by this focus' (Hoare, 2007, p. 268). Consequently, this lack of robust data renders this document of little value in terms of identifying worldwide fraud losses. Similarly, the *12th Global Fraud Survey* (Ernst and Young, 2013) also fails to offer a valid contribution to developing an accurate picture of losses for the very same reasons.

CIFAS

The longstanding annual publication *Fraudscape*, Credit Industry Fraud Avoidance System (CIFAS, 2011, 2012, 2013) records information on fraud cases that have been detected by CIFAS members, but does not provide a picture of overall fraud losses. Consequently, these data are only just considered guestimates, this being another output seeking to advertise the organization's services, and are of very limited value in providing an accurate picture of overall fraud losses.

Kroll

The Kroll (2009) *Global Fraud Report* has been included within this category because no detailed explanation of the measurement methodology is offered. The report advises that 'a total of 729 senior executives took part in the survey' (p. 2), but no detail provided about the questions asked, and what evidence the respondent's answers are based on. As a consequence, the finding that financial services fraud has increased by 18 per cent (p. 6) cannot be given any credibility because no data audit trail is provided.

The *Global Fraud Report* (KROLL, 2014) provides a combination of fraud-related articles but offers even less in terms of specific fraud loss data. The report's findings could be given more credence if there was more detail concerning the research methodology.

The charitable sector

Fraud in the charitable sector is a relatively new discovery; in fact the Charity Commission has not even begun estimate fraud within this sector (NFA, 2010a, p. 31). The first suggestion that charities are vulnerable to fraud was provided by the report on *Fraud in the Charitable Sector*, observing that 'the extent of fraud within and against charities in the United Kingdom is relatively unknown' (Fraud Advisory Panel, 2009, p. 4). The findings reveal that 7 per cent of survey respondents had been the victim of fraud within the last two years. The research methodology comprises of a self-completion postal survey and six detailed interviews. The response rate for the postal survey of 22 per cent suggests that the limited data acquired is insufficient to provide an accurate picture of the losses suffered by this sector.

The NFA (2011a, p. 18) advise that with over 180,000 charities registered with the Charity Commission, 'their focus for this year in quantifying fraud loss in the third sector has been on measuring fraud against charities'. Targeted measurement work involves the issue of a survey to 10,000 charities, and the responses received exceeding 1,000. Consequently, any data produced has to be treated with caution, when considering that the response rate of 10 per cent actually equates to 1 per cent of the total registered charities.

For the subsequent report, the NFA (2012) increased the size of the sample to 34,000 but achieved a lower response rate of 9 per cent. It is estimated that charities lose 1.7 per cent of their income to fraud, which equates to £1.1 billion. This figure is questionable because it also falls well below the average percentage of expenditure lost to fraud of 5.7 per cent (Button and Gee, 2013, p. 73). Further data giving cause for concern is that the 'vast majority of those surveyed believed that their organization was effective at preventing fraud' and that fewer than 4 per cent of respondents indicated that they had detected fraud (NFA, 2012, p. 21).

The estimate for the VC sector of £147 million (NFA, 2013, p. 21), which is a significant reduction from the 2012 estimate due to a change in the research design, also has limitations, being based on a response rate of just 6 per cent to an online survey of charities with an income of over £100,000 a year. This survey is also based on perception, with respondents being asked to estimate a percentage of their income lost to fraud that is undetected. I suggest that the significant reduction in estimated losses from 2012 may constitute a gross undercounting of losses.

The responses to both surveys raise some serious questions: first, are charities still being complacent about fraud, believing that it will never happen? Alternatively, is there an awareness that fraud exists, but reluctance to measure because any publicity might impact on donations? What is imperative however is that this sector acknowledges

DOI: 10.1057/9781137406286.0007

vulnerabilities to fraud and develops appropriate counter-strategies. Failing this, an alternative option would be to incorporate this sector in any mandating legislation. This may appear draconian, but a drive for increased measurement is in the interest of this sector because addressing losses will help compensate for lost donations resulting from the economic downturn.

Review of methodologies

This section offers a review of the analysis of fraud data outputs by producing a synopsis of the fraud measurement methodologies adopted by each organization.

Table 3.1 summarizes the multiplicity of fraud measurement data collection methodologies applied by the public and private sectors when attempting to measure fraud. It should be noted that UK Payments have been excluded because no detail of methodology was supplied in the document. Having conducted a detailed review, the statistically valid fraud data outputs considered to contain sound methodologies are those employing representative samples that stand up to rigorous academic scrutiny. Furthermore, the DWP who trail blazed the development of an improved measure of fraud losses has maintained data quality, thus presenting a starting platform for future development of best practice. Nevertheless, despite being at the forefront of fraud measurement, there is room for improvement within DWP processes. In contrast to the findings of the Fraud Review Team (2006, p. 31) that considered HMRC to have robust fraud measurement methodologies, this review finds otherwise. HMRC data are unreliable because certain measures are reliant upon third party data, whose validity is beyond their control.

There is also a significant lack of rigour in the loss data provided by many central government departments, evidenced by those that offer a nil return; equally, those that do measure fraud present data of very poor quality, mainly because they rely upon detected fraud, rather than conducting statistically valid sampling exercises.

Focusing on the private sector, insurance industry data are the only measurements that come anywhere close to standing up to academic scrutiny. Much of the private sector produced reports, such as those produced by Ernst and Young (2013) and Kroll (2014), are of limited

DOI: 10.1057/9781137406286.0007

TABLE 3.1 *Summation of fraud measurement methodologies*

	Count of detected fraud	Count of suspected fraud	Probability sample	Administrative data	Data matching	Literature review	Qualitative Interviews
Audit Commission	✓			✓			
BBC					✓		
DVLA		✓			✓		
DWP		✓	✓	✓			
FCO	✓			✓	✓		
HMRC	✓	✓	✓	✓	✓		
H M Treasury		✓					
MOD		✓					
NFA	✓	✓	✓	✓	✓	✓	✓
NHS		✓	✓		✓		
ABI	✓	✓		✓		✓	✓
BDO	✓						
CIFAS				✓			✓
Ernst and Young				✓			✓
KPMG	✓						
Kroll							✓
NERA	✓	✓		✓	✓		
Norwich Union	✓	✓		✓			

value due to the failings previously discussed. This research typology would be better replaced by measurement exercises conducted by each individual industry in the private sector, which at least would offer a worthy contribution to developing a more accurate picture of fraud losses.

In summary, the data presented within Table 3.1 enables the conclusion to be drawn that the recommendations contained within existing fraud measurement critiques about standardization have not been implemented. Specifically, it is worth noting that the NFA, who are perceived to produce the most accurate representation of fraud losses, actually employ all of the measurement methodologies within their annual indicator. I therefore conclude that, eight years on from the Fraud Review Team (2006), the need to improve the quality of fraud measurement now requires more assertive action based on the options for change advocated within this book. On a more positive note, this review has identified some good practice, which offers a starting point for the development of improved fraud loss measurement.

I close this section by suggesting that the varying methods employed to calculate fraud losses identified within this taxonomy evidence the need for a standardized method of loss measurement that is embraced by all organizations, and if necessary, mandated to ensure compliance.

Methodological deficiencies

Critical analysis of the measurement processes within the fraud data outputs reviewed, combined with content analysis of the limited critiques of fraud measurement, has identified recurring issues that need to be addressed to improve the quality, reliability and comparability of fraud loss data.

The reason for measurement was carefully considered while reviewing private sector fraud loss reports, particularly those produced by organizations that are not inwardly looking, that is to say, those that conduct organizational fraud loss measurement exercises, but fail to release data at national, sector or even industry level. When examining fraud loss data publications, this analysis has identified considerable variations in fraud loss figures, specifically estimates produced by private sector organizations vary significantly. This further evidences the unreliability of private sector loss measurement exercises that appear to be self-initiated, rather

DOI: 10.1057/9781137406286.0007

than underpinned by sector or industry sponsorship. To reiterate previous suggestions to improve accurate fraud measurement, organizations should only measure their own losses, unless specifically commissioned to do so, rather than produce commercially motivated data intended simply to create an organizational 'moral panic' (Cohen, 1972) to generate business. Kirk (2008, p. 335) offers an example, when citing a BDO report with the emotive headline 'as the credit crunch bites so do the fraudsters'.

While some reports provide interesting qualitative data, they offer little contribution towards the accuracy of fraud measurement within the UK. A pertinent example being the Ernst and Young (2006, 2013) reports which fail to offer any specific fraud loss data, rather sitting within the category of marketing documents, whose specific intention is to generate new business. While these types of documents are inevitable in the commercial world, I suggest that they offer no contribution towards offering a more accurate measure.

This type of research should be replaced by measurement exercises conducted by each individual private sector industry. Accordingly, these publications should be discounted when any improvements to measuring fraud are developed. They could be eradicated by the further development of an independently produced enhanced version of an Annual Fraud Indicator, sourcing data direct from those specifically measuring fraud within their own area of responsibility.

Frequency of measurement is another methodological deficiency requiring attention. For example, even though the DWP offer what this review considers to be the most statistically valid fraud loss data, there are certain inadequacies in these data due to the lesser frequency of measurement of certain benefits. To expand, although DWP has frequently reported substantial fraud losses (National Audit Office, 1998, 2008a), these data lack extant Disability Living Allowance (DLA) fraud data, this benefit last being measured in 2004 (DWP, 2005). This timescale is inadequate to provide accurate detail of total losses of DLA, a benefit frequently targeted by the greedy calculating or systematic fraudster (Tunley, 2010b, p. 14, 2011, p. 316), when compared with the rolling measurement of means tested benefits. I suggest that this may be explained by a perception that DLA losses are low and do not warrant such frequent measurement. Alternatively, due to the sensitivity and potential adverse publicity, a less rigorous approach is applied.

DOI: 10.1057/9781137406286.0007

There are other public sector organizations that conduct measurement exercises sporadically, one example being local authorities as evidenced by the Audit Commission (2010, 2011, 2013). The NFA (2010c) however do seek to address the infrequency of data compilation within the public sector by recommending that a more comprehensive estimate of fraud losses should be produced annually. Nevertheless, as evidenced, central government departments have continually ignored HM Treasury directives, so even with the backing of the Cabinet Office, what guarantee is there that these departments will fully comply with instructions issued?

Another obstacle to accurate measurement is the inconsistencies in defining what constitutes fraud (Levi and Burrows, 2008, p. 298). Yet the report (Levi et al., 2007) issued the previous year offers an estimate of overall losses drawn from 'hybrid' data using inconsistent fraud definitions. I therefore contend that if those charged with reviewing the process actually identify weaknesses, but then offer loss data that is based on such inconsistencies, then there is an urgent requirement for a standard definition for measurement purposes. I evidence this assertion using the observations of this review, which maintains that little progress has been made. To develop this theme further than previous reviews, this book now discusses the range of different fraud definitions identified.

Within the public sector for example, there are departments with bespoke counter-fraud legislation such as the DWP and HMRC, which although intended as a prosecution tool, are the criteria upon which loss measurement exercises are based. For example, the DWP normally prosecute benefit fraud under the Social Security Fraud Administration Act 1992. Thus when measuring fraud using common sampling, the DWP use this statute as an evidential test of whether fraud can be proved, but also use the benefit conditions of entitlement as a test to identify whether a claimant's declared circumstances are considered fraudulent. Interestingly, the NHS relies upon the civil definition of fraud (Keenan, 2007, pp. 320–321), based on case law (Derry v Peek 1889). Due to the range of functions performed by the NHS, there is no specific statute that prescribes conditions of entitlement; therefore drawing upon the common law to measure fraud is a reasoned decision.

Similarly, there is no consistent definition of fraud within central government departments; however Her Majesty's Treasury (2009a) do offer examples of the *modus operandi* of fraud typologies based on detected cases. In terms of measuring fraud in local government, the

Audit Commission offer their own 'bespoke' definition of fraud, which was discussed in Chapter 1. As discussed, the NFA's *Annual Fraud Indicator* is a 'hybrid' report that incorporates data based on varied definitions of fraud. If the concept of this report is to be further developed by any newly created independent measure, all data used must be based on one single definition of fraud, which would then enable comparative and longitudinal analysis of these data. Examination of private sector fraud measurement publications reveals that frequently there is no disclosure of the fraud definition upon which the measurement has been based on. Furthermore, many private sectors produced fraud loss reports rely upon criminal determination, drawing upon successfully prosecuted cases.

If there is no consistent definition of fraud within the public sector, then the likelihood of finding consistency among all sectors is extremely remote. The problem with an individually created definition of fraud however is that it can be both politically and commercially driven to influence the outcome of any measurement exercise. Consequently, an independently devised definition, possibly informed by academia, might prove to be the best solution.

This review has also identified a continuing failure to measure fraud accurately and consistently, hence the inclusion of the 'guesstimate' category. Analysis has identified the two principal deficiencies that limit the reliability of these fraud loss statistics; these being reliance upon apparently unsubstantiated third party data, and inconsistencies in data used. I will first address the problems of using data matching for the purpose of fraud measurement.

While many of the reports described as hybrids are reliant upon what may be described as an amalgamation of data from a range of sources, there are some measures that are dependent upon data matching using third party data. For example, the measurement of TV licence evasion (TV Licensing, 2009) combines two data sets, one of which is external data which presents problems when attempting to set a level of statistical confidence. Specifically, the importing organization has no control over the data collection and analysis, and consequently, if unclear from the data supplied, any statements of statistical validity may well have to be taken upon trust.

Furthermore, there is no explanation of how these data have been captured, and consequently their validity cannot be judged. It may be that in some instances these data are fit for purpose, for example means tested benefit records; therefore it is essential that there is a full and

DOI: 10.1057/9781137406286.0007

detailed explanation of methodology including an account of the statistical validity of all data used. I therefore suggest that if any organization has no alternative but to rely upon third party data, they validate its accuracy to ensure that any fraud loss measurement data stands up to the highest level of scrutiny.

For the purpose of this review, I define inconsistent data as any that originate from multiple sources and used in reports that have been categorized as hybrids. The principle issue with these reports blending data is that they are of significantly limited value, because harvesting data from a number of sources frequently results in a muddle of figures based on assorted data collection methodologies, varying time spans, different data typologies and inconsistent statistical validity.

Regrettably, the NFA's *Annual Fraud Indicator* falls within this category. The NFA are predominantly 'fraud data collection agents', and therefore reliant upon third party data. Consequently, the arguments presented earlier about the inadequacies of these data may apply to the fraud losses reported by the NFA because they have no option but to rely upon these figures. Based on this 'given', I suggest that the only option to ensure regular and accurate fraud measurement, at least in the public sector, is to mandate this activity and supply a common standard supported by a manual of guidance that offers 'best practice'.

There is also very limited rigour within the fraud loss data outputs evaluated. Levi and Burrows (2008, p. 296) observe that few studies on fraud emanate from academic sources. From the literature reviewed, this continues to be the case, there being no identified loss measurement exercises supported by academic input. Content analysis of the publications falling within the inclusion criteria has enabled the identification of specific shortcomings, all impacting upon the rigour of these fraud loss reports. The principle shortcomings identified by this review are detailed in Table 3.2.

One final methodological issue identified by this review is only relevant to the public sector, this being combining of fraud and error when conducting and reporting the results of measurement exercises, something that is still advocated by the FED Taskforce (Her Majesty's Government, 2012, p. 9). Both are entirely different, possessing diverse root causes and can be identified through a thorough examination of cases sampled. Consequently, there is no reason why they should not be measured and reported individually. In terms of the DWP, one explanation is that ministers have always sought to make political capital from

TABLE 3.2 *Summation of limitations of fraud loss reports*

	Purpose not explained	Lack of detailed method	Deficient research methods	Limited statistical confidence	Lack of clarity	Poor quality presentation	Lack of Informed Conclusion
Audit Commission		✓	✓	✓	✓		
BBC			✓	✓	✓	✓	
DVLA			✓	✓	✓		
DWP			✓	✓			
FCO	✓	✓	✓	✓	✓	✓	✓
HMRC			✓	✓	✓		
H M Treasury		✓	✓	✓	✓	✓	✓
MOD	✓	✓	✓	✓	✓	✓	✓
NFA			✓	✓	✓		
NHS					✓		
ABI			✓	✓	✓		
UK Payments	✓	✓	✓	✓	✓		
BDO	✓	✓	✓	✓	✓	✓	✓
CIFAS		✓	✓	✓			
Ernst and Young			✓	✓			✓
KPMG		✓	✓	✓			✓
Kroll		✓	✓	✓	✓		✓
NERA		✓		✓	✓		✓
Norwich Union			✓	✓	✓		✓

DOI: 10.1057/9781137406286.0007

social security fraud and combine fraud and error figures 'for dramatic effect' (Sainsbury, 2003, pp. 291–292). I therefore suggest that any legislation-mandating fraud measurement should direct organizations to separate fraud losses from error.

Review

This chapter commenced by examining the dark figure of fraud. Having discussed the literature inclusion criteria, the following section examined fraud measurement within all sectors by evaluating fraud data outputs, and reviewing critiques of existing fraud measurement methodologies. The issues identified are principally based on the frequent assumption that fraud may only be measured by examining reported instances or detected cases, and such exercises are labour-intensive and therefore costly. Furthermore, despite regular criticism of data quality, little remedial action has been taken in the form of collecting data fit for purpose, from which meaningful and comparable analysis may be conducted.

A thorough review of the literature has uncovered evidence which suggests that there is still much work to be done to improve fraud loss measurement by addressing the limitations identified in this chapter. Furthermore, in view of the matter-of-fact approach taken to fraud measurement and the reluctance to voluntarily address the deficiencies evidenced within this review, improvements in data quality and accuracy may only be facilitated by legislation-mandating fraud measurement.

DOI: 10.1057/9781137406286.0007

4
Measuring the Cost of Fraud

Abstract: *This is the first of three chapters presenting the research findings, and concentrates on the questions asked about measuring the cost of fraud. The chapter commences by profiling the survey respondents, offering a breakdown of representation by sector, individual position and organizational function. Verbatim responses from academics and fraud professionals to the question 'What do you define as fraud?' are then offered. The chapter then presents answers to the question on whether the respondent's organization measures fraud, followed by explanations offered on why organizations fail to measure fraud. Fraud measurement methodology is then discussed, before offering opinions on the ideal measurement frequency. The chapter closes with respondent's explanations about what fraud typologies are measured.*

Tunley, Martin. *Mandating the Measurement of Fraud: Legislating against Loss.* Basingstoke, Palgrave Macmillan, 2014. DOI: 10.1057/9781137406286.0008.

Respondent confidentiality

To maintain confidentiality, verbatim responses from interview respondents have been allocated the identifier of either 'A' (Academic) or FP (Fraud Professional), combined with a numerical identifier (e.g. FP1). Fraud professionals one and three represent the private sector, and the remainder the public sector. Similarly, responses harvested from the questionnaire 'free text' sections are reported in a manner that maintains participant confidentiality, while indicating the sector, industry or department, and where relevant but with no risk of compromise, the respondent's position. Finally, within all findings chapters, the 'voluntary/charitable' sector is represented as 'VC'.

The sample

Useable responses received, broken down by sector are detailed in Table 4.1. Those surveyed were then provided with the opportunity to disclose their position within the organization. There was a response rate of 60 per cent ($n = 111$), and the data provided suggests that the survey population represents a broad spectrum of fraud professionals as detailed in Table 4.2. Respondents selecting the 'other' option include owner, bursar, analyst, chief accountant, managing director, underwriter and lead auditor.

TABLE 4.1   *Please indicate which sector your organization falls within*

	n	%
Public	85	46
Private	68	37
Voluntary/charitable	32	17
Total	185	

TABLE 4.2   *What is your position in the organization?*

	n	%
Manager	31	17
Investigator	24	13
Head	15	8
Director	11	6
Senior	5	3
Auditor	4	2
Group	2	1
Other	19	10
No response	74	40

DOI: 10.1057/9781137406286.0008

TABLE 4.3   *What is your organization's function?*

	n	%
Local authority	21	11
Local government	16	9
Insurance	15	8
Welfare/benefits	11	6
Health	8	4
Banking/financial	7	4
Education	5	3
Care	3	2
Retail	2	1
No response	97	52
Total	185	

The 88 responses to the optional question concerning organizational function reveal that all major organizations and industries within the public and private sectors are represented (see Table 4.3). The VC sector has not been similarly sub-categorized, because identification at sector level is all that is required for this research. These data suggest that survey participants offer adequate representation of those involved in the fraud environment. While the sample size is small, they do represent the public sector, and private sector industries that are known to experience significant fraud losses, for example banking, retail and insurance. While there may be limitations on generalizability, in particular because the size of the organizations represented is not known, these data do provide some representation of opinion on fraud measurement from all three sectors.

What is fraud?

One of the historical issues hampering accurate measurement is the absence of a consistent definition of fraud for this purpose. This study therefore gathered data to help develop a definition of fraud that is specific, transferable and easy to understand by measurement practitioners. Fraud professionals and academics interviewed were asked to offer their definition of fraud which could be used for the purpose of measurement, which resulted in a range of opinion being offered, including some simply relying on the existing statute, thus confirming the difficulty in pinpointing a universal definition of fraud.

DOI: 10.1057/9781137406286.0008

However, not all were convinced that this legislation is suitable,

> the Fraud Act is as close as we come to having a good quality definition. It certainly makes it clear in your mind as to what's fraud and what's not fraud but it certainly doesn't help the person who is quantifying if the case should be counted as fraud for the purpose of measurement. (FP2)

An alternative view is that the civil definition is more appropriate for measurement purposes, offering both increased clarity and the opportunity to treat fraud as a business cost:

> If you have a criminal law definition then you are excluding some losses, which can be recovered and taken forward in civil law so we use the civil law concept of fraud which has been prevalent in this country since 1889 Derry v. Peak. (FP1)

Each interviewee did offer their own definition, some of which contained recurring themes worthy of consideration when developing a standard definition of fraud, as evidenced below:

> It is the obtaining of financial advantage or cause of loss by invisible expressive deception. It is the mechanism by which a fraudster gains unlawful advantage or causes unlawful losses. (A2)

> The deliberate misuse of circumstances with the intention of gaining some advantage. Or withholding information that should be given. (A4)

> It involves a false declaration, actus reus, with intent to deceive, mens rea. In terms of a criminal offence it involves dishonest intent to gain an advantage through a deception. (FP3)

Do you measure fraud?

It was important to identify the extent of existing fraud measurement within all three sectors. All survey participants were therefore asked to indicate whether their organization measures fraud (see Table 4.4). Within the sample, there is an active level of fraud measurement across

TABLE 4.4   *Does your organization measure fraud?*

	Public	Private	VC	n	%
Yes	60	49	14	123	66
No	25	19	18	62	34
Total	85	68	32	185	

all three sectors, with 66 per cent ($n = 123$) of all respondents answering 'yes' to this question. When analysed by sector, the private sector has the highest amount of measurement activity within the organizations represented, this being 72 per cent ($n = 49$).

When drilling down to the micro level however, some very interesting and significant responses are identified. For example, the fact that 29 per cent ($n = 25$) of respondents from the public sector responded 'no' to this question does suggest that there is still a lack of commitment within the public sector to fully embrace fraud loss measurement. Of particular relevance, is that of these 25 respondents, seven indicated that they were from local authorities and another five declared their organizational function as local government. What is noteworthy is that the declared role within their organizations indicates a spread of functions including fraud manager, risk manager and senior auditor. However, it is somewhat paradoxical that organizations spending public money create such posts, but neglect to measure fraud. The survey further reveals that there are central government departments that fail to measure fraud.

Turning to the private sector, one surprising discovery is that while the ABI are creating an Insurance Fraud Register documenting proven fraudsters, two insurance industry respondents indicated that their organization fails to measure fraud. Other examples of no fraud measurement within parts of the industry include retail and manufacturing. The results from the VC sector reveal that 56 per cent ($n = 18$) of respondents indicated that no fraud loss measurement takes place. While the response rate from this sector was low, this still provides a starting point for estimating the extent of fraud measurement within this sector, and suggests that fraud awareness needs to be increased, including educating charitable organizations on the financial benefits of regular measurement.

Why no measurement?

To gain an understanding of business culture and mindset, those respondents indicating that their organization did not measure fraud were asked to provide an explanation of why this is so. The 75 responses to this question offer some interesting data:

▸ 11 respondents from the private sector, seven from the VC sector and one from the public sector advised that there is no fraud in their organization.

DOI: 10.1057/9781137406286.0008

▸ Two public sector, one private sector and three VC sector respondents suggested that their organization did not need to know.

▸ Four public sector, five private sector and three VC sector respondents indicated concern about adverse publicity if the results were publicized.

▸ Two respondents from the private sector indicated that it was to protect shareholders interests

▸ The remaining 36 respondents gave 'other' reasons

One noteworthy explanation offered within the other category is that:

> because we are a religious charity there is no fraud.

Paradoxically, the most significant question raised by these responses is that if organizations do not measure losses, how can they be certain there is no fraud?

There are two possible explanations for these data, first a continuing lack of fraud awareness within the private and VC sectors, and second a reluctance to accept the existence of fraud, generated by fear of the impact such an admission might create. This latter suggestion is supported by the survey respondents who indicated concern about adverse publicity from releasing such information. This issue however, could be addressed by being seen to rectify the situation. To ensure all organizations measure fraud, let alone to a predetermined standard of accuracy, may require implementation of some persuasive strategies, particularly when noting that respondents from all sectors indicated that their organization had no need to be aware of fraud.

When exploring the 'other' responses offering an explanation why organizations do not measure fraud, there are certain answers that suggest senior management complacency and failure to grasp the full impact of fraud. For example, a chief executive of a charity explains that:

> given the nature of my organization, significant fraud is unlikely. Low level fraud is inevitable but we can live with it.

Another pertinent response offered by the head of internal audit from a charity indicates that fraud measurement,

> Is seen as a low priority because the level of fraud is perceived to be low and it is so difficult to gain an accurate measurement.

This suggests there is an urgent need to educate the VC sector about fraud risks.

DOI: 10.1057/9781137406286.0008

Within the public sector responses there is evidence of a continuing reluctance by certain departments to acknowledge that fraud exists and should be measured. One explanation for lack of activity is offered by a local authority fraud manager, who reveals that,

> Senior management and/or elected members are ambivalent towards fraud and corruption.

A similar response is offered by a local government fraud services manager, who succinctly advises that fraud is not measured because there is,

> no interest!

This suggests there is a need for a directed strategy towards educating senior local government managers about managing and measuring fraud. Lamentably, there appears to be a reduction in terms of fraud measurement within certain healthcare trusts, one fraud specialist revealing that

> Other priorities are considered more important.

This response is disappointing when considering the previous work undertaken centrally within the NHS to measure fraud.

Reluctance to measure is also present within central government, as evidenced by the response from a manager within the department charged with regulating the public sector who reveals that:

> the focus tends to be on measuring fraud in organizations we regulate rather than our own.

Another illuminating response is from a manager working within the legal aid department, who explains that fraud is not measured due to,

> concern about adverse publicity if results made public.

This reluctance to confront the fraud problem offers additional credence to the argument for mandating measurement through the creation of a statute, while also educating senior managers on the business benefits by using a knowledge transfer and best practice exchange network as the conduit. While the cabinet office may have some authority, issuing directives recommending measure does not fully address the lack of activity within central government departments.

This book has also identified a comparable level of complacency within the private sector. While the issue of no fraud present has already been discussed within this chapter, of interest is the equally paradoxical

DOI: 10.1057/9781137406286.0008

response from the managing director of a private sector fraud investigation company who reveals that fraud is not measured because there is

> no fraud in the organization.

Further empirical evidence of private sector complacency towards fraud measurement is provided by the head of fraud training from an insurance company who discloses that;

> Although the organization undertakes fraud work for other organizations there is little concern that fraud may be occurring within.

A further revelation, which suggests a culture of responsibility for fraud measurement needs developing, is provided by an insurance industry counter fraud officer, who maintains that,

> Fraud is not the responsibility of one area and therefore there are no consistent factors to enable the effective and accurate measurement of fraud costs or savings across the business.

Immoral phlegmatism?

At this point, I consider it worthwhile to discuss the attitudes to fraud measurement, both individual and organizational, as evidenced so far. Within the sample, assuming that this is a barometer of opinion within the wider population, there are a significant number of organizations within all three sectors which fail to see fraud as a problem at all, or are reluctant to accept the actual size of the problem.

Regular perusal of newspapers suggests that the media have a limited interest in fraud, the exception being benefit fraud. Whereas media representations of certain crimes, for example violent crime and youth offending, often exaggerates 'certain risks' (Newburn, 2007, p. 93). This style of media representation resulted in the development of the concept of a 'moral panic' (Cohen, 1972), which occurs when 'a condition, episode, person or group of persons become defined as a threat to societal values and interests' (Cohen, 1980, p. 9). This equanimity towards a crime typology costing the UK '£52 billion per annum' (NFA, 2013, p. 2) is in direct contrast to that described by Cohen (1972, 1980, 2002).

In the context of fraud, this divergent reaction prevalent among top decision makers that fraud is not a problem and the response to it adequate is defined by this research as *immoral phlegmatism*. Something

DOI: 10.1057/9781137406286.0008

immoral is described as 'being wrong or bad' (Alvarez, 2010, p. 93), or even 'hostile to the welfare of the general public' (Words and Phrases, 1959, p. 226). This ambivalence and lack of interest by management towards the fraud problem described by respondents, which dispassionately allows the loss of public funds to go unchecked in times of austerity, is indeed *immoral phlegmatism*.

A pertinent observation is offered by Kleinman et al. (2011, p. 56), who argue that 'institutional immorality will indeed shake the basic ethical values'. Accordingly, the unethical decision by financial service and insurance institutions to recover fraud losses from the consumer rather than addressing the problem, combined with survey responses suggesting little concern the fraud is occurring within some private sector organizations offers further examples of *immoral phlegmatism*. This culture also permeates through the VC sector, with survey respondents suggesting that the fraud risk is perceived as being low, and some organizations 'can live with it'. Drawing upon the aforementioned definition, I suggest that it is immoral that charitable organizations ignore the risk of fraud, thus potentially allowing the money from public donations to be stolen by fraudsters rather than reaching the intended recipients.

The reluctance to view fraud as a serious business risk is also in direct contrast to the concept of deviancy amplification, whereby an act of deviancy is considered worthy of attention and 'responded to punitively' (Cohen, 2002, p. 8). This phlegmatism among decision makers within all three sectors can be linked to a number of factors. First the fraud problem goes through a process of de-labelling, it is not measured appropriately, and as a result, insufficient resources are allocated to dealing with the problem. This circular process of attenuation of the problem creates feedback to reinforce this 'spiral of decline'. The approach to this problem by decision makers can be influenced further by a naïve belief in the attenuated problem before them, or more seriously, that it is in their commercial interests not to confront the problem. The consequence of this phlegmatism however, whether through naïvity or commercial interest, is an immoral response to fraud in state institutions and many organizations (Button and Tunley, 2014).

This complacent attitude to fraud is actually an international issue. Turning to the US, and evidence concerning the financial crisis, the National Commission on the Causes of the Financial and Economic Crisis in the United States (2011) clearly demonstrates there was much concern in organizations at the scale of the fraud problem. However,

DOI: 10.1057/9781137406286.0008

those decision makers in a position of power to define the response failed to act, even though signs of the coming crisis were there several years before its impact. News reports suggested mortgage fraud was an increasing problem, yet little or no action was taken to ward off the impending crisis.

Accordingly, the build up the financial crisis in the US and the reaction to it has been phlegmatic. There has been denial and under-estimation of the size of the problem, and given the damage it has caused to the financial sector and wider society, this response is immoral.

The results from the NFA's (2013) private sector perception survey also provide empirical evidence to support the argument of *immoral phlegmatism* being developed within this book. The fact that certain private sector businesses refused to participate in the perception survey using the argument that 'they had no fraud' even after being advised that 'their input was critical' (p. 62) could suggest a reluctance to acknowledge the existence of fraud and measure losses. I draw this conclusion based on the inference that, if they already measured fraud, it is unlikely that they would refuse to participate.

The attitudes towards fraud defined as *immoral phlegmatism* suggests that, in addition to developing the options for change, there is a need to cultivate an attitude adjustment whereby fraud is allocated the business priority it requires.

Is measurement important?

This question was posed to interviewees and survey participants. The questionnaire responses are presented in Table 4.5. The responses indicate a high level of support for accurate fraud measurement, with 59 per cent ($n = 109$) considering it 'very important' and 94 per cent considering it either 'important' or 'very important' ($n = 174$). Analysis of responses by sector reveals that there is no difference between the two principal sectors, with 62 per cent of respondents from each indicating that the accurate measurement of fraud is 'very important', whereas only 44 per cent of VC sector respondents selected this response. When combining these responses with those selecting the 'important' option however, 91 per cent of respondents from this sector fall within these two categories ($n = 29$). While only a small sample, this does suggest that there is some acknowledgement within the VC sector that measuring fraud is important.

DOI: 10.1057/9781137406286.0008

TABLE 4.5   *How important do you think the accurate measurement of fraud is?*

	Public	Private	VC	n	%
Not important at all	0	0	1	1	1
Not important	1	0	0	1	1
Neither important nor not important	4	3	2	9	5
Important	27	23	15	65	35
Very important	53	42	14	109	59
Total	85	68	32	185	

This project also obtained opinion on the importance of measuring fraud, commencing with the public sector (see Table 4.6). These data suggest collective opinion recognizes the need to measure public sector fraud losses, with 73 per cent of respondents considering it 'very important'(n = 135) and 97 per cent believing it to be either important or very important (n = 179). Responses by sector are very similar, with 96 per cent of respondents from the public sector selecting the 'important' or 'very important' options (n = 82), compared with 97 per cent from the private (n = 66) and VC sectors (n = 31). Table 4.7 presents opinion on the importance of measuring fraud within the private sector.

The opinion of all respondents reveals that only 48 per cent consider it to be 'very important' (n = 88), this figure rising to 92 per cent when incorporating those who selected 'important' (n = 169), which suggests some level of support for measuring private sector fraud. Interestingly, a higher proportion of public sector respondents (94 per cent) consider it to be either 'important' or 'very important' (n = 80), compared to 90 per cent in the private sector (n = 61) and 88 per cent in the VC sector (n = 28). The views on measuring fraud within the VC sector are presented in Table 4.8.

A total of 63 per cent of all respondents (n = 116) considered measurement to be 'very important', which is 15 per cent higher than responses selecting this option in respect of the private sector. When adding those indicating it to be 'important' this increases to 96 per cent (n = 177), which is 1 per cent lower than the views on the importance of measuring public sector fraud, but 4 per cent higher than responses relating to the private sector.

Interview participants were asked their opinion on the importance of fraud loss measurement when developing fraud strategies, with collective opinion believing it to be essential to underpin counter measures with

DOI: 10.1057/9781137406286.0008

TABLE 4.6   *How important do you think it is to measure fraud in the public sector?*

	Public	Private	VC	n	%
Not important at all	0	0	0	0	0
Not important	0	0	0	0	0
Neither important nor not important	3	2	1	6	3
Important	17	15	12	44	24
Very important	65	51	19	135	73
Total	85	68	32	185	

TABLE 4.7   *How important do you think it is to measure fraud in the private sector?*

	Public	Private	VC	n	%
Not important at all	0	0	0	0	0
Not important	0	1	0	1	1
Neither important nor not important	5	6	4	15	8
Important	34	27	20	81	44
Very important	46	34	8	88	48
Total	85	68	32	185	

TABLE 4.8   *How important do you think it is to measure fraud in the voluntary/charitable sector?*

	Public	Private	VC	n	%
Not important at all	0	0	1	1	1
Not important	0	0	0	0	0
Neither important nor not important	3	2	2	7	4
Important	25	23	13	61	33
Very important	57	43	16	116	63
Total	85	68	32	185	

reliable accurate data. For example one fraud professional maintains that fraud measurement is,

> essential, because if you don't know the nature of the scale of the problem how on earth are you going to put in place the right solution? (FP1)

Collective academic opinion offers a similar viewpoint,

> It is imperative that fraud is measured accurately so that it provides a yardstick of the success of counter strategies. (A5)

> If you can't measure the success or evaluate what you've done to any degree of certainty ... you can't verify whether there was value for money in that or whether this is actually working. (A1)

accurate data enables you to stop people committing fraud and prevents the media from making it up. (A4)

How do we measure fraud?

This survey sought data on the different methodologies applied when measuring fraud, seeking to identify commonalities, which might inform a cross sector standard of measurement. It was also important to identify examples of fraud being only partially measured, thus failing to capture the full extent of potential losses. Table 4.9 illustrates responses by sector from the 123 participants who indicated that their organization measures fraud.

Survey data reveals that the organizations represented are predominantly reactive in terms of fraud measurement, with 65 per cent (n = 200) indicating that measurement regularly focuses on detected cases rather than sampling. It should be noted that multiple responses were permitted, thus illustrating that some organizations represented adopt a combined approach, using both methodologies.

The percentage of confirmatory answers to this question (excluding 'other') by sector is reported in Table 4.10, offering an insight into organizational practise within the sample. If it is accepted that this survey

TABLE 4.9   *How does your organization measure fraud?*

	Public	Private	VC	n	%
Received incidents of fraud (detected) by number of cases	51	42	11	104	34
Received Incidents of fraud (detected) by total monetary value of losses	45	44	7	96	31
Fraud loss measurement exercise by number of suspected cases	21	21	5	47	15
Fraud loss measurement exercise by total monetary value of suspected losses	19	20	3	42	14
Other	9	6	1	16	5
Total	145	133	27	305	

TABLE 4.10   *Percentage proactive/reactive approaches to fraud measurement by sector (based on confirmatory responses)*

	Public (%)	Private (%)	VC (%)
Reactive	71	68	69
Proactive	29	32	31

DOI: 10.1057/9781137406286.0008

offers a measure of opinion within the wider population, this prevalence of a reactive approach to fraud measurement within the organizations represented, must be addressed if a more accurate representation of fraud losses is to be achieved.

Analysis of free text responses from survey respondents also reveals a leaning towards reactivity, evidenced by the response from a public sector team leader, whose organization's measurement methodology adopts the following process,

> Every single example of fraud is rigorously checked and recorded for both numbers, type and financial loss.

Similarly, a public sector fraud prevention and detection manager suggests that measurement is reactive, advising that,

> We also include a measure of frauds prevented because of checks we have in place.

There is some evidence of common sampling to inform loss measurement, as evidenced by a head of financial services from the public sector, who indicates that in addition to loss measurement, the department conducts

> Systematic compliance checks ... in high risk areas.

Maintaining the good practice previously established, responses indicate that the NHS are still conducting some loss measurement exercises at the micro level, as evidenced by a 'regional anti-fraud lead' who reveals that they conduct,

> locally run measurement exercises.

How often should we measure fraud?

Having established that collective opinion acknowledges the importance of measuring fraud, the optimum frequency of these loss measurement exercises is also pertinent. The answer to this question is likely to be determined by the way organizations use their fraud loss data, the comparative costs of measurement against losses, and organizational turnover or budget.

When examining the frequency of loss measurement exercises within the sample, the preference appears to be for yearly exercises. Table 4.11 presents details of the percentage of respondents from each sector indicating which typology of measurement exercise their organization conducts annually. These data reveal that within the VC sector organizations sampled, there is less inclination to measure fraud on a regular basis.

Having established that within the sample, organizational preference is for annual exercises, this chapter will now present the opinions of questionnaire and interview respondents on the ideal measurement frequency. Table 4.12 presents data reporting the opinion of those sampled on the most appropriate intervals between fraud loss measurement exercises. The response to this question is relatively conclusive, with 74 per cent of respondents (*n* = 137) indicating that, in their opinion, fraud should be measured annually. Responses by sector demonstrates some consistency in opinion favouring measurement annually, with the public sector being most positive at 75 per cent (*n* = 64), and the least positive being the VC sector, although still demonstrating a large proportion, this being 72 per cent (23).

The 27 questionnaire participants selecting the 'other' option also offer some informative data, with responses suggesting a wide variation in preferred measurement timescales. Interestingly, some respondents

TABLE 4.11   *Percentage of fraud measurement exercises by typology conducted annually by sector*

	Public (%)	Private (%)	VC (%)
Received incidents of fraud (detected) by number of cases	69	73	42
Received incidents of fraud (detected) by total monetary value of losses	70	76	33
Fraud loss measurement exercise by number of suspected cases	58	64	50
Fraud loss measurement exercise by total monetary value of suspected losses	65	62	42

TABLE 4.12   *How often do you think fraud should be measured?*

	Public	Private	VC	n	%
Annually	64	50	23	137	74
Every two years	11	8	2	21	11
Other	10	10	7	27	15
Total	85	68	32	185	

DOI: 10.1057/9781137406286.0008

suggest that measurement frequency should vary by sector. For example, a private sector senior fraud analytical consultant argues that,

> Fraud should be measured as often as possible – in the public sector this is monthly as there is a direct impact on the financial performance of the organization. In the private sector, the systems and processes are geared towards fraud prevention rather than fraud detection. However, in the insurance sector, this is more akin to public sector due to the lengthy investigation time and the 'claim' being the focus rather than the insurance policy (think of national insurance as a home insurance policy and a incapacity claim as a home insurance claim).

The above response is interesting, specifically the comparison between fraud detection processes within public sector benefit delivery and the insurance industry in terms of dealing with 'claims'. This suggests that both organizations might learn from each other's best practice, which could be facilitated by a knowledge transfer forum incorporating all sectors.

One refreshing response from the VC sector indicates some awareness of the need to measure fraud consistently. Interestingly, the respondent recommends shorter intervals, suggesting that,

> this should be a continuous measure – monthly would be appropriate and then an annual review as well.

A further pertinent observation is offered by a local authority head of audit, observing that,

> the frequency would depend on the reason why you are trying to measure fraud in the first place and how accurate the measurement is likely to be.

The key objectives for measuring fraud are to identify risk and subsequently implement a control strategy, which can then be evaluated. If an organization considers the principal aim of re-measurement is to utilize new loss data to assess the impact of strategies informed by an earlier exercise, frequency may be determined by what is a realistic timescale for these to impact.

This however, is only one rationale of regular fraud measurement, an equally important principle being the identification of new emergent risks, which then inform future control strategies. Accordingly, the frequency of measurement should not be linked to detection, but informed by the knowledge that fraudsters are always developing new *modus operandi*, and infrequent measurement exercises could enable these to become lost or embedded within organizational processes. In sum, there are varying reasons why fraud is measured, and it is important to set a realistic frequency that meets business needs, but responses suggest that annual exercises are the preferred option.

One final survey response is offered in support of the contention that directed strategies are required to progress VC sector fraud measurement. The respondent, a finance director of a VC organization, remarks that frequency of measurement is

> a matter for stakeholders to decide, shareholders, trustees etc.

Nevertheless, when an organization is reliant upon public donations, it does have a corporate responsibility, aside from any moral or ethical obligation, to ensure all donations are used for the intended purpose and not lost to fraudsters.

The opinion of interview respondents reveals unreserved agreement that loss measurement exercises should be conducted annually. This collective opinion is summed up by one academic, who advises that,

> measurement frequencies have to be realistic, but annual exercises would be the most appropriate as demonstrated by key public sector departments. (A6)

What is measured?

This chapter will now examine what is measured by each sector. Table 4.13 details fraud typologies measured by each sector. It should be recognized that because this question offered multiple selection options, the

TABLE 4.13   *What types of fraud does your organization measure?*

	Public	Private	VC	n	%
Overall losses	40	37	8	85	46
Customer fraud	45	42	7	94	51
Procurement fraud	31	19	8	58	31
Payroll fraud	29	18	8	55	30
Expenses/subsistence fraud	29	21	10	60	32
Major company expenditure	9	15	9	33	18
Other internal fraud	33	22	7	62	34
Other	12	9	2	23	12
No answer	25	19	18	62	34
Total potential responses for each variable	85	68	32		

DOI: 10.1057/9781137406286.0008

total will not be consistent with the number sampled by sector. It should also be noted that 62 respondents offered no answer to this question, which equals the number of respondents indicating that their organization does not measure fraud. These data suggest there is consistency in what is measured within the VC sector, the array of responses falling between eight and ten for each specified category.

Unsurprisingly, the public and private sectors concentrate on overall losses and customer fraud, whereas the most frequently measured typology within the VC sector is expense and subsistence fraud, which indicates that other significant risk categories are not addressed, while also suggesting a need to educate senior managers in fraud risk awareness.

One typology which responses indicate may be measured consistently by each sector is procurement fraud, signifying there is at least some level of risk awareness present within each sector. Analysis of responses also suggests a requirement to increase the number of exercises measuring internal fraud within public and private sector organizations.

Review

This chapter has presented research findings that support the contention that it is essential organizations measure fraud losses accurately, and at a consistent and appropriate frequency. Furthermore, many respondents indicate that annual measurement is the optimum frequency for fraud loss measurement exercises. Explanations have been offered about why certain organizations fail to measure fraud. This attitude has been defined as *immoral phlegmatism*, which has been evidenced by indifference and complacency toward the fraud problem. Details of what typologies are measured within each sector have also been outlined, which is of value when developing a standard measure.

The chapter also sought answers to the question '*what is fraud?*', upon which a persuasive consensus of opinion has not been achieved, although some commonalities have been identified.

DOI: 10.1057/9781137406286.0008

5

Legislating Fraud Loss Measurement

Abstract: *This chapter presents the research findings on mandating the measurement of fraud through legislation. The chapter commences by discussing opinion on mandating fraud loss measurement and the possible arguments that may be offered against such a proposition. The focus then moves to the creation and implementation of a statute and whether this legislation should prescribe what fraud is measured, how it is measured, and the frequency of measurement exercises. It also considers the release of what may be sensitive data into the public domain. The chapter closes with a discussion of arguments against the proposed creation of a statute mandating measurement, and evaluates the reasons offered why this is not considered a feasible option.*

Tunley, Martin. *Mandating the Measurement of Fraud: Legislating against Loss.* Basingstoke, Palgrave Macmillan, 2014. DOI: 10.1057/9781137406286.0009.

Mandating measurement

The next section of the survey sought respondent's opinions on the creation of a statute mandating fraud measurement, and what they consider the potential arguments against this proposal might be. Table 5.1 presents opinion on legislating fraud loss measurement. The results presented reveal that just over three quarters of survey respondents are supportive of a statute mandating fraud measurement. Interestingly, the highest level of support emanates from the private sector, with 85 per cent of those sampled answering in the affirmative ($n = 58$), as opposed to 69 per cent (public sector) ($n = 59$) and 75 per cent (VC sector) ($n = 24$). Should these participant responses be representative of the wider population, the creation of such a statute would have the support of practitioners, which may be used to influence decision making at ministerial level.

This question was also posed to interviewees, with one respondent offering a very positive response to this question, demonstrating knowledge of US legislation, arguing that, if a statute was being considered, it should be,

> Something like the IPIA. As long as the detailed guidance is right it will be great for the public sector, and for the private sector it will be the best route for the government to change accounting standards. (FP1)

Table 5.2 presents the arguments against mandating fraud that survey respondents suggested may be offered. Cost and bureaucracy are considered to be the most likely arguments against the creation of a statute. This attitude to what has been demonstrated as a high value crime nationally, may only be addressed by developing a culture whereby fraud is seen as a problem that needs to be addressed. It should therefore be treated as a business cost, which can be reduced through regular measurement, the application of informed control strategies and pursuing recovery of identified losses, thus ensuring savings exceed costs.

TABLE 5.1　*Should a statute be created to mandate fraud measurement in the UK?*

	Public	Private	VC	n	%
Yes	59	58	24	141	76
No	26	10	8	44	24
Total	85	68	32	185	

DOI: 10.1057/9781137406286.0009

TABLE 5.2   *Arguments against mandating fraud measurement*

	Public	Private	VC	n	%
None	7	6	1	14	3
Current measurement statistically valid	13	23	2	38	9
Do not need to measure fraud losses so accurately	16	11	9	36	9
Too bureaucratic	59	51	25	135	33
Too costly	69	52	24	145	35
Other	21	17	3	41	10
Total	185	160	64	409	

Survey participants offering individual responses have also provided some valuable data. One public sector respondent suggests that to encourage fraud measurement, a change in attitude is required, observing that,

> Fraud measurement has traditionally been used as a stick to beat organizations with (think DWP). There needs to be a cultural change to make fraud measurement a positive experience.

This view is offered in support of the argument presented in this book that there should be no stigma attached to an admission that fraud exists within an organization as long as there is evidence of positive steps being taken to address the problem. This could include creating a risk register, developing an investigative resource or changing processes to reduce vulnerability. This suggested cultural change would help address the *immoral phlegmatism* previously discussed.

Further support for mandating measurement is offered by a public sector financial investigator who suggests that central government may be reluctant to mandate public sector fraud measurement due to,

> Potential political embarrassment and the desire to conceal the truth.

This belief supports the contention that while appearing to promote public sector fraud measurement, in reality, previous governments may not have been fully committed to this strategy. Unfortunately, there is currently insufficient evidence on the activities of the Coalition's Counter Fraud Taskforce to make an informed decision on the present government's commitment to improving the accuracy of fraud loss measurement. Until there is an acceptance that more than just detected fraud can be measured, there is a risk that nil returns will continue to be submitted by central government departments.

DOI: 10.1057/9781137406286.0009

The opinion of a local government head of audit also suggests that there may be resistance within the private sector to mandating fraud measurement, manifesting itself in the form of,

> Lack of co-operation from private sector e.g. fear of adverse publicity.

A regional head of fraud in the private sector offers another potential counter argument, identifying that potential commercial compromise may generate resistance because of,

> sensitive information that an organization may be unwilling to disclose.

Continuing this theme, an explanation for this reluctance to disclose these data within the private sector is offered by a senior fraud analytical consultant, who suggests that,

> the private sector sees fraud as a commercial, competitive issue.

A further concern is offered by an insurance industry compliance manager, who observes that,

> Data created would be sensitive or subject to misuse.

These are valid concerns because fraud loss data may be commercially sensitive and release may have an adverse impact on a company, such as a reduction in share value for example.

The following observation offered from a public sector respondent recognizes these concerns, thus highlighting the need to address the uneasiness within the private sector over publication of fraud loss data:

> the private sector and in particular financial institutions, would regard such measurements, if published, as a risk to their business and competitively damaging.

Before developing this discussion further, I offer two contrasting responses that reject the mandating of fraud measurement. The first is from an audit manager from the VC sector, who indicates that internal organizational procedures may remove the need for specific measurement exercises, contending that,

> Internal procedures may cover this requirement.

The second, is offered by a private sector investigations manager who presents a very negative view on fraud measurement, posing the questions:

> What value does it add? What use will it be? May have an adverse affect on a company standing?

DOI: 10.1057/9781137406286.0009

These opinions further illustrate an urgent need to address *immoral phlegmatism* through cultural change that embraces accurate fraud loss measurement. Furthermore, in support of the argument for mandating the measurement of fraud outside the public sector, this book contends that it is unethical for private sector businesses to make good fraud losses by transferring these costs to the customer; something which the insurance industry has admitted is common practice. Similarly, it is even more important during a period of financial constraint that charities ensure that losses to fraud are kept to a minimum.

When developing such a policy however, one important consideration relevant to all sectors is organizational size and capability to comply with directives from such a statute, a view offered by a public sector manager who argues that,

> Mandating will not be fair on all organizations. Account needs to be taken of their size, resources and vulnerability to fraud.

A similar opinion is offered by a public sector team leader, who suggests that,

> loss is very different across different sectors. To hold my own organization to the same criteria as a bank or a charity would simply not work as we are completely unique and have little in common with other sectors.

These comments are of particular relevance when considering how fraud measurement could be mandated, what should be measured, and which organizations or even sectors might be included. Accordingly, outside the public sector, organizational size and annual turnover should be determining factors, and an appropriate de-minimus limit established which is realistic in terms of which organizations it encapsulates.

Proactive measurement

Of concern is the finding that many survey participants consider that detection is the only fraud loss indicator. To address this, work is required to develop a cultural change in approaches to fraud measurement including a better understanding of options such as common sampling, and the development of a mindset accepting that, anticipating fraud and changing processes, is a more cost effective option than existing prevention and detection methods. The following response from a chief executive in the VC sector is offered in support of this argument for a cultural change:

> It would be better to put money into improving methods of detecting and countering fraud.

Unfortunately, this view suggests a limited understanding of the value of accurate fraud measurement. For example, how does an organization know what to counter and what strategies to develop if it is not measuring? I offer a similar opinion from a local government manager:

> Can only measure known fraud – impossible to quantify unknown (successful?) fraud. So stats are meaningless.

Once again, this exemplifies the limited understanding of what can be measured through the use of statistically valid sampling, and suggests that there is a need for a directed educational strategy on measuring fraud and the associated business benefits. In support of this argument the views of one interviewee are offered, who contends that,

> it's important for people to start thinking of fraud as a cost and understanding that all fraud losses can be measured. I guess we just need to get that information out there. The more that can be got out to people, the more they understand. (FP1)

Creating a statute

The research then sought respondent's views on the creation of legislation mandating the measurement of fraud and whether this is considered to be the only means of ensuring accurate and consistent measurement. The views of survey participants are presented in Table 5.3.

TABLE 5.3   *Arguments against the creation of a statute*

	Public	Private	VC	n	%
Fraud measurement should be voluntary	6	6	1	13	13
Current measurement statistically valid	5	0	3	8	8
Do not eed to measure fraud losses so accurately	3	1	4	8	8
Too bureaucratic	19	8	7	34	33
Too costly	17	8	4	29	29
Other	6	3	1	10	10
Total	56	26	20	102	

DOI: 10.1057/9781137406286.0009

Interestingly, while this question offered the similar option of multiple answers, the total responses to the fixed choice answers are considerably lower than the previous question. An inference that may be drawn is that there may be fewer arguments presented against the creation of a statute mandating fraud than just a policy change attempting to enforce compliance with a new process. The generalizability, is however somewhat limited, because these data represent only 24 per cent of the sample ($n = 44$), these being the respondents who do not agree with the creation of a statute.

The perceived counter arguments against creating a statute are again bureaucracy and cost. These recurring themes are relevant to all sectors involved, however the financial benefits of measurement and re-measurement exercises should outweigh any costs. This is particularly important in times of government spending cuts, as identified by a public sector fraud manager who suggests that,

> protecting public funds is very important, Government cut backs on staff resource will make this increasingly difficult in the future.

While embracing the importance of advocating fraud measurement, the issue of cost is again raised by another manager from the public sector, who suggests that,

> Whilst it would be useful to encourage fraud measurement in high risk areas in other areas the costs may outweigh the benefits.

The issue of costing is particularly relevant to small and medium private sector enterprises, however, when considering the estimated fraud losses of £780 million (NFA, 2011a, p. 36) experienced by these businesses, some form of positive action to measure fraud is required. To address the issue of cost implications, I draw upon the opinion of one interviewee, who suggests that,

> You don't want to spend lots of money measuring fraud, but you do want to spend the right amount so that you end up with a good quality figure that allows you to justify all the other spend on fraud prevention and detection. (FP2)

Therefore, any statute introduced may have to incorporate different standards of measurement for private and VC sector organizations, possibly based on annual turnover or number of staff employed. A mechanism for implementing such a directive is offered by one academic, who contends that,

> something akin to a national code of practice would be essential. With rankings so you can have three levels of quality. Such as, this is the highest

quality data. This is the lowest quality because you only met this many quality standards. One kite mark but different rules that you adhere to depending on the type of data that you're collecting. (A1)

The following response also identifies the need for a flexible measurement standard, which in turn may generate increased compliance. The view offered being that,

> if we just have one standard then some people will shy away from it. They need to have some options to choose. (FP1)

These observations are significant, and while relevant to the creation of a statute, also offer an informed view on how a British Standard of fraud measurement could be framed.

When developing a statute, it is important to emphasize that significant returns on investment can be achieved by regular measurement exercises; therefore costs will be offset by reduced business losses. In support, I offer the response of one interviewee, who contends that,

> Think of it as an investment, and a return on the investment. You have to think about the cost of the work as the investment and then look at what you get back from it. If you are measuring accurately you can see the loss figure coming back because fraud hasn't happened. (FP1)

Another positive view is offered by an academic who argues that creating a statute is,

> the only way forward to ensure proper and accurate fraud loss data. (A3)

A slightly more reserved opinion is offered by a fraud professional who maintains that,

> I think argue for it, but I think we should give people a chance to do this optionally first in the private sector, see where we get. (FP2)

In terms of bureaucracy, this is a recurring argument levelled at government; however, this can be addressed by educating organizations on the financial benefits of regular fraud measurement. Although this may not negate the need for legislation, it will at least go some way to challenge what is perceived as officialdom.

Finally, of interest is a contrasting response from an interviewee, who again raises the issue of commercial sensitivity, revealing that,

> I am not persuaded immediately that compulsory legislation is needed for the public sector. I would need to think about it more. When considering

DOI: 10.1057/9781137406286.0009

the private sector, I have a real problem with the commercial sensitivity of data. (A4)

The issue of sensitivity may be addressed within the private sector by requiring organizations to demonstrate compliance, permitting them to keep resultant data out of the public domain, but supplying it for anonymized inclusion in any national measure.

This chapter will now explore the opinions offered on which sectors should be incorporated into legislation mandating fraud measurement. Table 5.4 reports the opinions of survey participants who have previously indicated they are in favour of a statute. Responses indicate that 99 per cent ($n = 140$) of participants favouring the creation of a statute suggest that this should be applied to the public sector. What is noteworthy is that a higher proportion of respondents are in favour of applying such a statute to the VC sector as opposed to the private sector.

Interestingly, with the exception of the public sector, there is limited support for the inclusion in the proposed statute of the sector from which respondents emanate. In fact only one-third of the respondent's from the private sector indicated that they were in favour of the proposed statute applying to this sector. Similarly, respondents from the VC sector offer limited support for this sector being incorporated into the statute, with only 46 per cent ($n = 11$) being in favour.

Interviewee responses also indicate a high level of support for the creation of a statute. There are however, differing opinions on which sectors this legislation should apply to. Initially, two opinions are offered suggesting that it should be applied to both the public and private sectors:

> I would basically say that if there was gonna be legislation then it would have to apply to both the public and private sectors. (FP5)

> It could become legislation that relates to the public sector, but surely everyone should be equally accountable, and just because you're making money rather than serving the public good doesn't mean that you should be held to a different account. You'd be lucky to get it passed as legislation in regards to the private sector but if there was enough pressure from the right places you could. (A1)

TABLE 5.4   *Which sectors should this proposed legislation apply to?*

	Public	Private	VC	n	%
Public sector	59	57	24	140	99
Private sector	40	19	7	66	47
Voluntary/charitable sector	51	42	11	104	74
Total potential responses for each variable	59	58	24	141	

DOI: 10.1057/9781137406286.0009

Another positive response offered with regard to mandating public sector measurement, which arguably also supports the proposed information exchange matrix and development of doctrine, the interviewee suggesting that,

> Yes you mandate it as it will help them benchmark themselves against other departments, but provide support, make it work for them. (FP1)

Another view is that the public sector is a good starting point, and compliance would put pressure on the private sector to embrace this concept, one interviewee arguing that,

> the public sector is a very good start and then the private sector might think, well that seems to be working. So rather than compelling them, if they see the standards of measurement are better, and the figures more accurate, they may conclude that we should follow that model. (A2)

However, the consensus of opinion is that mandating public sector fraud measurement may be a realistic option, but incorporating the private sector may be one step too far, this being illustrated by the following response:

> I believe that a statute would be a positive move in terms of the public sector as it would ensure transparency within all departments. It may prove difficult to persuade the private sector to publish results, but at least persuading them to measure accurately and then do something about it is important. So why not include them in the statute but include in the drafting something that says they have to measure but they only have to demonstrate to somebody, not sure who, that they have measured. (A5)

In relation to these sectors, one further viewpoint is offered, suggesting that the proposed legislation should be restricted to the public sector, maintaining that,

> I believe that the creation of a statute may be the only option to develop an accurate national picture which can then inform a national control strategy. This should be limited to the public sector if it has any chance of being passed as legislation. There is a chance that with MPs having connections to the private sector it is unlikely that ministers would be willing to support such a bill if the private sector were included which might the put at risk the chances of it being passed for the public sector. (FP4)

Finally, while the initial interview schedule only raised the issue of mandating fraud within the public and private sectors, there were certain respondents who demonstrated an awareness of the evolving issue of fraud and its impact on the VC sector. While not supporting the incorporation of this sector within any proposed statute, it was suggested that there is an urgent need for a fraud measurement strategy that embraces this sector in some manner. One interviewee observing that,

> Charities need to maximise every penny they receive so measuring fraud is important. It may prove sensitive to legislate that they measure but perhaps they could be persuaded in some way to embrace this idea. (A5)

Legislating measurement: when, what and how?

Frequency of measurement has already been discussed in the context of organizational policy; this section will now consider the appropriate measurement frequency for mandatory exercises. Subsequently, the views of survey respondents on the extent to which a statute should specify what is measured and the methodology to be applied will be reported.

Table 5.5 details the responses from those sampled by instrument on the frequency of measurement. The responses from the 141 respondents in agreement with the creation of a statute suggests that there is little doubt that annual measurement is considered the ideal frequency with 79 per cent ($n = 112$) of respondents offering a response selecting this option.

The preferred frequency for fraud measurement exercises suggested by interviewees is also annually, as evidenced by the following responses:

> Annual makes sense to me. You want to look at your other types of cost annually; you need to know what your forecast is annually. (FP1)

> Annually sounds quite sensible for specific fraud measurement exercises. (A4)

> On an annual basis, particularly if you are looking at detail changes over time. If you're trying to have an impact then that kind of regularity in measurement is essential. (A1)

TABLE 5.5 *How regularly should mandated fraud measurement exercises be conducted?*

	Public	Private	VC	n	%
Annually	42	49	21	112	79
Every two years	15	8	2	25	18
Other	2	1	1	4	3
Total potential responses for each variable	59	58	24	141	

Interestingly, some interviewees justified the selection of annual data collection by arguing that the requirement to measure should be linked to both the development and subsequent evaluation of control strategies, and the identification of themes, risks and patterns. Moreover, this offers evidence to support the argument that to develop accurate measurement, there needs to be consistency to ensure comparability. The pertinent views of two fraud professionals are that:

> Measuring fraud annually provides sufficient frequency to track the impact of new strategies without leaving too much of a gap that enables new frauds to target the organization. (FP6)

> Annual is reasonable. Monthly would be too much of a burden, every two years seems a bit infrequent for fraud measurement to look at trends which in turn will inform counter measures. (FP2)

To enable fraud losses to be treated as a business cost, an identical frequency of measurement should be applied to these data that is used to measure all other costs falling within this category. One interviewee actually raises this point, suggesting that,

> most companies report annually, most government departments report annually so I think annually is definitely the best so that fraud losses can be included in annual reports. (A2)

Directing measurement

Table 5.6 illustrates further responses from the 141 respondents in agreement with the creation of a statute. Interestingly, the responses to this question indicate a level of support for legislation being authoritarian, with 84 per cent ($n = 118$) of the 141 participants offering a response in the affirmative.

The same 141 survey participants were then asked whether this legislation should influence any measurement methodology. The findings are

TABLE 5.6   *Should legislation prescribe what types of fraud are measured?*

	Public	Private	VC	n	%
Yes	46	51	21	118	84
No	13	7	3	23	16
Total potential responses for each variable	59	58	24	141	

DOI: 10.1057/9781137406286.0009

documented in Table 5.7. The results are not dissimilar to the preceding question, with 80 per cent (*n* = 113) of the 141 participants responding to the question indicating that they believe a statute mandating fraud measurement should include a directive on the methods to be employed when conducting such exercises.

Reporting findings

This section explores opinion on publishing fraud loss data, commencing with views on whether this should be mandatory. Data in Table 5.8 reveal that there is even more support for the publication of fraud loss data, with 92 per cent (*n* = 130) of the survey respondents favouring the creation of a statute indicating that they believe the resultant data should be released. The highest level of support is offered from public sector respondents, 97 per cent (*n* = 57) being in favour, compared to 90 per cent (*n* = 52) from the private sector and 88 per cent (*n* = 21) from the VC sector.

Responses from interviewees also generated some informative views. For example, one fraud professional when discussing the US IPIA, suggested that apart from mandating measurement, the statute has other commendable features relating to the public sector, specifically,

> All of the information has to be published so that the public can see it, get angry and increase the pressure to reduce it. It's the level of transparency and accountability that makes it powerful, not just the measurement. (FP1)

TABLE 5.7   *Should legislation prescribe what fraud measurement methodology is employed?*

	Public	Private	VC	n	%
Yes	47	48	18	113	80
No	12	10	6	28	20
Total potential responses for each variable	59	58	24	141	

TABLE 5.8   *Should legislation also mandate the publication of fraud loss data?*

	Public	Private	VC	n	%
Yes	57	52	21	130	92
No	2	6	3	11	8
Total potential responses for each variable	59	58	24	141	

DOI: 10.1057/9781137406286.0009

Collective opinion however, offers less support for mandating the publication of private sector fraud loss data with the recurring theme of commercial implications being offered as the principal reason for these data being retained in confidence. The response detailed below is offered as an example of these shared views.

> Commercial sensitivity is important to consider when debating the publication of private sector data. (FP3)

Interestingly, one academic offers a potential solution, suggesting that,

> An external group could validate the measurement, reviewing and checking that some form of consistent standard has been applied. Legislation that enables these validation teams get access might be sufficient. (A1)

A statute could compel the private sector to measure to a British Standard, present their data and the NAO or an independent academic institution could then adopt an auditing role and publish a certificate of validation, similar to that mandated in the Sarbanes–Oxley Act 2002, which proves the legislation has been complied with. These data may then be incorporated into any existing fraud loss indicator, with organizational identities remaining in confidence.

Opinion was also sought on what the perceived risks to publishing fraud loss data might be. This question offered fixed choice answers but also provided a 'free text' option. The results are documented in Table 5.9. The results are yet again unsurprising; with 89 per cent ($n = 125$) of the 141 participants in favour of creating a statue offering a response indicating that organizational embarrassment is considered to be the most likely reason for resistance to publishing data. When examining data at sector level, interestingly 93 per cent ($n = 55$) of participants from the public sector offering a response indicated that organizational

TABLE 5.9   *What are the perceived risks to publishing fraud loss data?*

	Public	Private	VC	n	%
None	1	2	5	8	6
Organizational embarrassment	55	51	19	125	89
Ministerial embarrassment	44	38	11	93	66
Commercial risk	31	35	4	70	50
Protection of shareholder's interests	25	29	4	58	41
Protection of head of organization	19	14	7	40	28
Other	9	4	4	17	12
Total potential responses for each variable	59	58	24	141	

DOI: 10.1057/9781137406286.0009

embarrassment is the most likely reason that might be offered in resistance to publication, compared to 88 per cent ($n = 51$) of private sector respondents and 79 per cent ($n = 19$) representing the VC sector.

The collective opinion of interviewees also suggests that organizational embarrassment is a prevalent culture that needs addressing. For example, one respondent maintains that,

> yes there is embarrassment, particularly in the public sector. Nobody wants to be the person to admit that substantial public funds are going astray. But the first stage to solve a problem is to stop being in denial about it. (FP1)

This fear of organizational embarrassment is also prevalent within the private sector and likely to be linked to company stability and the potential impact on share value. An issue identified by two interviewees:

> There is obviously going to be an element of organizational embarrassment within the private sector. Particularly when management have to answer to shareholders. (FP6)

> Private sector companies may well be embarrassed by the publication of fraud losses. Mainly because of the commercial impact in terms of share value and market confidence. (A5)

These responses further support the earlier contention that measurement may be mandated by statute that incorporates the public and private sectors, but compulsory publication of data limited to the public sector. Private sector companies could be allowed to obtain a certificate of validation to prove compliance. This could even be applied to some of the very large VC sector organizations, once they have been persuaded to measure.

Review

This chapter has presented findings suggesting there is some support within the sample population for mandating fraud measurement, while also identifying potential arguments against such a proposal. The dogmatic and equanimous arguments offered against such a proposal from some respondents have been cited as additional evidence of *immoral phlegmatism* towards the fraud problem.

Opinion has also been presented relating to the creation of a statute, and to which sectors this should be applied to. Respondent's views reveal more support for creating a statute mandating fraud measurement in the

DOI: 10.1057/9781137406286.0009

public sector than in the remaining two sectors. The views of all respondents have also been documented relating to the mandatory publication of fraud loss data. These indicate a high level of support for releasing public sector data, but opinion was cautious about the publication of loss data from the private and VC sectors.

DOI: 10.1057/9781137406286.0009

6
The Doctrine of Fraud Loss Measurement

Abstract: *This chapter initially examines the level of statistical confidence of fraud measurement data disclosed by questionnaire respondents. The focus then moves to the creation of a British Standard of measurement. When considering the value of this option for change, its feasibility will be examined at both macro and micro levels. This chapter then explores the creation of an information-exchange and knowledge-transfer infrastructure to develop core doctrine of fraud loss measurement, including the participation in this process by organizations from all sectors.*

Tunley, Martin. *Mandating the Measurement of Fraud: Legislating against Loss.* Basingstoke, Palgrave Macmillan, 2014. DOI: 10.1057/9781137406286.0010.

Reliability of measurement

The findings presented in the previous chapters indicate that fraud losses are measured by certain organizations within all sectors. While acknowledging this is good practice, it is imperative that these data accurately reflect losses and can be validated accordingly. This research therefore posed the question '*How accurate do you consider current fraud loss data to be?*' to all interviewees. The majority indicated that they have limited confidence in fraud loss data; the following two responses being offered as an example of this viewpoint:

> Not very accurate due to the iceberg phenomenon. (A3)

> The reality of it is, despite many reports identifying the same issues, very little progress has been made in terms of improving accuracy to a reliable level. (A6)

Two participants did offer an opinion on reliability by sector, observing that:

> There's no doubt that in terms of accuracy, data produced by some public sector organizations that do measure is relatively accurate. Because the private sector has a commercial agenda, there is always a concern that this may compromise accuracy. (A5)

> The public sector has got more accurate information than the private sector. Overall measurement would have been a lot further advanced in the NFA if the British Banking Association hadn't been so nervous about not wanting everything properly measured. (FP1)

These observations suggest that there may be a need to create some form of standard measure to which all organizations comply. This will address the issue of uncertainty surrounding the accuracy of some fraud loss data, particularly that produced by some private sector organizations.

The opinion of two interviewees does raise some concern about exactly how much progress in improving accuracy of measurement has been achieved, with both placing limited value on data produced by the National Fraud Authority:

> Based upon data I have seen I don't think the NFA data is terribly accurate. (FP1)

> Some data will stand up to scrutiny such as DWP and NHS. I do have concerns though about some of the combined loss data such as that produced by NERA. Likewise I am cautious of NFA data. The overall loss data produced, when you actually read their report, doesn't come across as being particularly

DOI: 10.1057/9781137406286.0010

accurate. You are left with the impression that as long as they receive something that can be added to their running total, they are not too fussy about how it has been measured. (FP5)

These final two responses offer additional evidence that if credible fraud loss data is to be produced, either by individual organizations or as a collective measure such as that produced by the NFA, it is imperative that consistency is achieved. This may only be attained by the creation of a universal standard of measurement.

Statistically valid measurement?

Table 6.1 presents responses from the 123 survey respondents indicating that their organization measures fraud about the level of statistical confidence these fraud loss data carry. The level of response to this question, whereby 40 per cent (n = 49) of the 123 respondents who had previously indicated that their organization does measure fraud were unaware of the level of statistical confidence applied to their organization's fraud loss data, is a little disappointing, but not unexpected because the survey instrument was circulated via a gatekeeper. Consequently, some respondents, while offering valuable opinion, may not be fully conversant with the complete fraud measurement process applied by their organization. Alternatively, the number of responses selecting 'do not know' may be a reflection on the limited value placed upon fraud measurement by the respondents, or that fraud loss measurement is not considered a priority by their organization. On a positive note however, these data do indicate that the 49 respondents are actually aware that fraud loss measurement does take place, and thus potentially afforded some priority within their organization.

TABLE 6.1   *What is the level of statistical confidence of your organization's fraud loss data?*

	Public	Private	VC	n	%
Between +/-1%and 4%	13	8	1	22	18
Between +/-5% and 9%	7	18	0	25	20
+/-10% or above	3	1	2	6	5
No statistical confidence	7	11	3	21	17
Do not know	30	11	8	49	40
Total	60	49	14	123	

DOI: 10.1057/9781137406286.0010

A total of 74 respondents were aware of the level of statistical confidence carried by the data produced by their organization. Within these responses, 38 per cent (n = 47) indicated that the level of statistical confidence was below +/–10 per cent, with only 18 per cent (n = 22) of respondents indicating it to be between +/–1 per cent and 4 per cent. Of further interest is that of those 74 respondents demonstrating an awareness of this figure, 21 participants representing all three sectors revealed that there is no statistical confidence in their organization's fraud loss data. What these responses do reveal however, should they be representative of the wider population, is that there is some reliability in extant fraud loss data, but much additional work is required to improve the robustness and consistency of these data cross sector.

When suggesting potential arguments against mandating fraud measurement, some survey respondents provided observations more relevant to this chapter. In particular, concerns have been expressed that statistical validity standards might be used as an argument against mandating fraud measurement. Some views are not unexpected, for example an internal auditor, a group chief accountant and a chief executive officer from the VC sector collectively suggest that it is not essential to measure fraud losses so accurately.

I accept that when developing a loss measurement strategy, the requirements of each sector are different, as highlighted by a manager in retail banking who suggests that there are:

> Too many variables across different industry sectors – could have a core mandatory reporting in line with CIFAS guidelines but would need to allow flexibility across all sectors. For public sectors, important that there is some consistency across fraud to public funds.

A similar view is offered by a public sector fraud manager who observes that:

> How you measure fraud will depend on the area that you are looking at – so quality, frequency, etc. of measurement will be determined by that and what is possible in some areas will simply not be possible in others. Therefore, whilst having some general principles to guide fraud measurement would be useful, it would be very difficult for prescriptive in all potential areas.

These are not acceptable rebuttals, because many organizations deal with a variety of fraud types. Certainly, one important means of addressing these refutations on the ability to measure consistently throughout all three sectors is through the development of a universal definition of fraud which is incorporated into any benchmark of measurement. This British Standard could inform both what is measured and how it is measured, and there is no reason why it could not contain classifications that are applicable to all organizations within all three sectors.

The views of interviewees were also sought on the ideal level of statistical confidence of fraud loss data. Those canvassed offered varying opinions; however there was some collective agreement that there does need to be an elevated level of confidence carried by fraud loss data. Two pertinent opinions being:

> You want it to the 1 per cent plus or minus. (A2)

> It's possible to be very accurate. Individual exercises that have taken place around the world can be very accurate with high levels of statistical confidence. Plus or minus 1 per cent in Europe. Outside Europe and the US plus or minus 2.5 per cent is the standard with 95 per cent statistical confidence outside the US and 90 per cent in the US. (FP1)

Conversely, one respondent was more relaxed about accuracy levels suggesting that:

> There should be tolerance of plus or minus 10 per cent. (A3)

A final viewpoint worth discussing is that from an academic who argues that there are more important considerations than just a figure when attempting to judge the reliability of data, the contention being that:

> You have to understand how the meta-data is collected, what it represents and what you think the strengths and weaknesses are. I think this approach is more valid than getting caught up in percentages. (A1)

These responses are of value when developing a standard of fraud loss measurement, because there is scope to combine high levels of accuracy and statistical confidence with a robust data collection methodology based on common sampling that offers both confidence in the process and the reported figures.

Creating a standard

Before developing a British Standard measure, it was important to canvass reaction to such an important criterion of measurement. Table 6.2 therefore presents the views of those sampled on this important criterion of measurement. These data reveal a satisfactory level of support

DOI: 10.1057/9781137406286.0010

TABLE 6.2   *How important is the creation of a British Standard of fraud measurement?*

	Public	Private	VC	n	%
Not very important	3	1	2	6	3
Not important	1	1	3	5	3
Neither important nor not important	17	6	10	33	18
Important	44	40	13	97	52
Very important	20	20	4	44	24
Total	85	68	32	185	

for the creation of a British Standard of fraud measurement, with 76 per cent ($n = 141$) of all respondents considering it to be either 'important' or 'very important'. The sector offering the highest level of support was the private sector, with 88 per cent ($n = 60$) of respondents indicating that they believed it to be either 'important' or 'very important', compared to 76 per cent ($n = 64$) of public sector respondents and only 54 per cent ($n = 17$) from the VC sector. The lower percentage response rate from the VC sector arguably offers further evidence of the need to develop increased awareness of the value of accurate fraud measurement.

Similarly, the majority of interviewees were in agreement, proffering the view that a British Standard would be a positive move towards improving the accuracy of measurement data. One participant suggesting that:

> I do think having a standard would be helpful. It's good practice, not best practice and in my ideal world the British Standard means that you do statistical sampling. (FP2)

A similar viewpoint offered being:

> Having a kind of gold standard and agreed set of definitions that an industry will sign up to makes sense. So we know that this bank has lost this much money through fraud. Also if you've got a comparable measurement across banks then surely that's an incentive to get more industry wide cooperation and understanding. (A4)

An additional argument presented is that the creation of a British Standard could guarantee data integrity, and without a prescribed standard, data quality would become:

> Discretionary, and all statistics would be unsafe. (A3)

Looking further ahead, having developed a British Standard, this could be developed into an International Standard. One interviewee

DOI: 10.1057/9781137406286.0010

suggesting that:

> A global standard should be defined because I don't like the idea of countries going their own way because then you don't have comparability. (FP1)

Survey participants also offered an opinion on this topic. Of particular interest is the response from the head of fraud in a banking organization, who acknowledges the business benefits of statistically valid fraud loss measurement exercises by revealing that:

> The Banking industry has agreed fraud measurement definitions for many fraud types, and shares data via UK Payments so a BS would not add too much value to Banking. That said, the data captured by banks really demonstrates the power of accurate measurement.

Before concluding this aspect of the research findings, two observations that may be considered supportive of this project are documented. The first interviewee, when discussing developing a standard of accurate measurement, observes that:

> Yes you are on the right lines in terms of the questions you ask about measurement. The biggest problem in measurement is how you achieve consistency of measurement. (A3)

The second response is even more specific, suggesting that:

> If we were to try and develop a British Standard, it probably should be somebody from academia. That way you would develop something that wasn't just a commercial project. (FP1)

Furthermore, the same participant believes that the research proposals are attainable, suggesting that combining all proposals, the ideal outcome would be a statute mandating measurement, supplemented by secondary regulation in the form of:

> A UK IPIA British Standard instrument about how to implement it, and then a validation agency to ensure that the measurements have been conducted. (FP1)

The fraud loss calculation

There are varied opinions on what should be incorporated into any fraud loss calculation, with some respondents suggesting that unequivocally prevention and detection costs should be included. First, the responses of two interviewees in favour of this methodology of loss calculation are offered, the first participant, when asked if prevention and detection costs should be included, advised:

> Yes definitely, but the problem is calculating the cost and data description should be specific about what has been included. (A3)

The second noteworthy response, while supportive of the inclusion of these costs, raises the question of public sector accountability, suggesting that:

> Having data on the cost of prevention and detection would be useful and would increase our understanding of what value for money we are getting from public sector counter fraud organizations. All would be useful to inform more sensible policy making. (A4)

There are however, differing opinions, one argument being that:

> Whilst costs of prevention and detection are important when looking at budgets, they are not specifically fraud losses. By including prevention and detection costs you are creating data that does not offer a true reflection of the actual monetary losses that have been experienced as a result of individual or group fraudulent activity, which are the most important data. (A6)

Having considered the arguments for and against, it is feasible that these costs may be offset by fraud that is prevented, because having weighed up the perceived risk of detection the potential fraudster decides not to pursue this activity. These costs should therefore be excluded from any fraud loss measures, although inclusion in accounts as a business cost would be appropriate.

Adopting the standard

Table 6.3 details the responses from survey participants on whether their organization would adopt such a standard. These responses suggest that there is a need to educate organizations about the value of a consistent and accurate measure. The positive response is relatively encouraging, with 55 per cent ($n = 101$) of those surveyed indicating that a British Standard of measurement would be adopted by their organization. This does however fall significantly below the 76 per cent ($n = 141$) of respondents who indicated that they considered the creation of a British Standard of value. These data might be explained by the fact that certain organizations may be represented by more than one respondent, and

DOI: 10.1057/9781137406286.0010

TABLE 6.3   *Would a British Standard of fraud measurement be adopted by your organization?*

	Public	Private	VC	n	%
Not likely at all	4	2	3	9	5
Likely	6	4	5	15	8
Neither likely nor unlikely	23	22	15	60	32
Likely	35	30	7	72	39
Very likely	17	10	2	29	16
Total	85	68	32	185	

thus there is no direct correlation between both datasets. What is of note however is that the affirmative responses of 61 per cent (*n* = 52) (public sector) and 59 per cent (*n* = 40) (private sector) offer more encouragement for advocating the adoption of a prescribed standard measure.

The affirmative response rate to this question of 28 per cent (*n* = 9) of VC sector representatives is disappointing, but unsurprisingly given the reluctance to confront fraud and embrace its measurement. This attitude has contributed towards the development of the concept of *immoral phlegmatism* within this research project. These data, while only being a small sample, suggest that there may be a need to develop a better understanding of the value of fraud measurement within this sector. It is therefore worth considering alternative options to mandating the publication of organizational loss data from this sector, due to fear of adverse publicity influencing the reluctance to embrace measurement and adopt a universal standard.

A further question was then posed within the questionnaire, seeking opinion on which sectors any British Standard should be applied to. The results are documented in Table 6.4. These responses signify that accurate fraud measurement is considered to be most important within the public sector, with 98 per cent (*n* = 182) of all respondents indicating that a British Standard of measurement should be applied. Interestingly, the fact that 86 per cent (*n* = 160) of respondents indicated that such a standard should be applied to the VC sector and 69 per cent (*n* = 127) considered it appropriate to the private sector offers further persuasion that this option for change is worth progressing. The higher response in respect of the VC sector could be explained by the fact that respondents recognize the important role that charities perform, particularly during a time of austerity. Opinion by sector reveals that 99 per cent (*n* = 84) of public sector respondents and 100 per cent (*n* = 68) of private sector

DOI: 10.1057/9781137406286.0010

TABLE 6.4   *Which sectors should a British Standard of fraud measurement be applied to?*

	Public	Private	VC	n	%
Public sector organizations	84	68	30	182	98
Private sector organizations	73	38	16	127	69
Voluntary/charitable organizations	79	56	25	160	86
Total potential responses for each variable	85	68	32	185	

respondents indicated that in their opinion, a British Standard of fraud measurement should be applied to the public sector. The responses concerning the private sector suggest limited support for imposing such a standard, particularly from private and VC sector respondents, who actually offer more support for applying this to VC sector organizations.

The consensus of opinion of interviewees is that a British Standard of Measurement should be embraced by all sectors, one respondent arguing that:

> A British standard of measurement is a good idea if it was applied by all sectors. Fraud data would then have more credibility. (A6)

Another participant, supportive of such a standard measure, raises the importance of comparability, suggesting that:

> A British Standard would enable more accurate longitudinal studies to be conducted. Simply because you would be able to compare like for like. (A5)

Finally, one important observation is that there should be more policing of the fraud measurement process, specifically that:

> If there was a consistent standard of measurement that was adopted by organizations, and more importantly, insisted upon by the NFA, then the data available would facilitate better informed decision making. (FP4)

Mandating standards

Tables 6.5–6.7 document the views of survey participants on mandating compliance with any British Standard of measurement within each sector. These data indicate that 85 per cent (*n* = 157) of respondents believe that compliance with a British Standard should be mandatory within the public sector, thus suggesting that this option for change should be progressed. Of note however is that those representing the

TABLE 6.5   *Should compliance with a British Standard be mandatory within the private sector?*

	Public	Private	VC	n	%
Yes	65	65	27	157	85
No	20	3	4	27	15
No answer	0	0	1	1	1
Total	85	68	32	185	

TABLE 6.6   *Should compliance with a British Standard be mandatory within the private sector?*

	Public	Private	VC	n	%
Yes	41	27	9	77	42
No	43	39	20	102	55
No answer	1	2	3	6	3
Total	85	68	32	185	

TABLE 6.7   *Should compliance with a British Standard be mandatory within the voluntary/charitable sector?*

	Public	Private	VC	n	%
Yes	56	49	14	119	64
No	28	18	16	62	34
No answer	1	1	2	4	2
Total	85	68	32	185	

private sector (96 per cent) ($n = 65$) and the VC sector (84 per cent) ($n = 27$) exceed the percentage emanating from the public sector (76 per cent) ($n = 65$). This indicates a significant level of concern that public funds may be at risk from fraud, and thus the implementation of a structured standard of measurement is worth pursuing.

Moving on to consider the private sector, the level of support within those sampled is significantly lower, with only 42 per cent ($n = 77$) of respondents indicating that such a standard should be mandatory within this sector. The level of support by sector differs, the highest percentage of respondents by sector originating from the public sector with 41 of the 85 respondents (48 per cent) answering in the affirmative.

Data relating to the VC sector indicate a more positive stance, whereby 64 per cent ($n = 119$) of respondents indicated that compliance with a British Standard should be mandatory. When examining responses by sector, this overall figure is skewed by the lowly 44 per cent ($n = 14$) of

DOI: 10.1057/9781137406286.0010

VC sector respondents answering in the affirmative, compared with 66 per cent (*n* = 56) of public sector and 72 per cent (*n* = 49) of private sector respondents. Arguably, this further supports the inference that there is a reluctance to embrace fraud risks within the VC sector.

Before exploring the development of core doctrine, in support of the argument for open and transparent fraud measurement, an observation is offered suggesting losses may be concealed by certain private sector industries, the respondent arguing that:

> Banks will often call a lot of their mortgage fraud, losses. They will not call it fraud, it's just impairment, they will settle it as bad debt. (FP2)

Developing 'best practice'

Survey participants were asked what value they placed on the creation of an information and best practice exchange matrix, and if their organization would participate in such an infrastructure. The opinions on the creation of such a network are reported in Table 6.8. These data represent a positive response to the creation of a knowledge-management infrastructure, with 80 per cent (*n* = 149) of all respondents considering it either 'important' or 'very important'. The views of representatives from the public and private sectors are also promising, with 86 per cent (*n* = 73) of public sector and 84 per cent (*n* = 57) of private sector respondents selecting either of the aforementioned options. The opinion of VC sector respondents is also encouraging, with 59 per cent (*n* = 19) selecting the same two options. Assuming this is a barometer of opinion, it offers a good starting point in terms of support for incorporating this sector in any fraud measurement knowledge-transfer process.

TABLE 6.8   *How important is the creation of a knowledge-management infrastructure for sharing best practice?*

	Public	Private	VC	n	%
Not important at all	1	0	2	3	2
Not important	1	1	0	2	1
Neither important nor not important	10	10	11	31	17
Important	45	41	18	104	56
Very important	28	16	1	45	24
Total	85	68	32	185	

Interviewees collectively supported the development of best practice, one example response being:

> I certainly think there is an argument made for good practice, and I think that should be made readily available. (FP2)

The development of this concept should be driven by a specific, but impartial organization, the same respondent suggesting that:

> I do think an organization like the National Fraud Authority should act as a repository for good practice, where people can access it as a resource. (FP2)

In view of the decision to close the NFA, this aforementioned role could be taken on by an academic institution.

The collective views reported suggest that the development of doctrine and sharing of good practice would garner support. What equally important however is that ownership of this proposed strategy is allocated, and the organization charged with this responsibility should be impartial and actively encourages participation.

The responses to the question on the likelihood of respondent's organizations participating in such a process are detailed in Table 6.9. The total 'positive' response by only 53 per cent (n = 97) of those sampled is somewhat disappointing, but it should be noted that the overall response figure is lowered by the fact that only 25 per cent (n = 8) of VC sector respondents answered positively.

The responses from participants representing the remaining two sectors suggest that this option for change is worth developing further. Specifically, 60 per cent (n = 51) of public sector respondents and 56 per cent (n = 38) of private sector respondents indicated that their organization would participate in a knowledge-management infrastructure.

TABLE 6.9   *Would your organization participate in a knowledge-management infrastructure?*

	Public	Private	VC	n	%
Not likely at all	1	1	3	5	3
Not likely	5	2	7	14	8
Neither likely nor unlikely	28	27	14	69	37
Likely	36	29	7	72	39
Very Likely	15	9	1	25	14
Total	85	68	32	185	

DOI: 10.1057/9781137406286.0010

Finally, one interesting response offered earlier in the questionnaire, but of relevance to this discussion, is provided by a representative from the insurance industry, who suggests that:

> Some businesses operate in a silo mentality and do not see fraud as a shared problem.

If this attitude is replicated throughout the industry, then it casts doubt upon the effectiveness of the ABI as a conduit for information exchange. Equally, if this is representative of the private sector in general, then I suggest that it evidences a need to educate this sector on the sharing of good practice and further supports the need for some form of knowledge-transfer matrix that is open to all sectors.

Review

This chapter has presented the views of those sampled on the subjects of reliability of fraud measurement data, including the level of statistical validity, the creation of a British Standard of fraud measurement and the development of a knowledge-management infrastructure. The findings suggest that collective opinion believes that there is an urgent need to improve the statistical validity of fraud loss data. Equally, there is a high level of support for the creation of a standard measure of fraud losses from those sampled representing the public and private sectors. The views of participants of both data collection methodologies also support the proposal to develop doctrine which is supported by the creation of an information-exchange matrix. Further evidence of *immoral phlegmatism* towards accurate fraud measurement has also been presented.

DOI: 10.1057/9781137406286.0010

7
Conclusion

Abstract: *This book has explored the theme of developing a more accurate measure of fraud, commencing with the critical position that to achieve this, certain criteria and processes have to be put in place. This chapter will explore the key enablers for the development of a more accurate measure of fraud, including mandating the measurement of fraud, the creation of a British Standard of fraud measurement and the development of a knowledge-exchange infrastructure. The initial focus of this chapter, however, will be the phenomenon of immoral phlegmatism and the need to facilitate a cultural change in attitudes towards fraud, and more specifically its measurement.*

Tunley, Martin. *Mandating the Measurement of Fraud: Legislating against Loss.* Basingstoke, Palgrave Macmillan, 2014. DOI: 10.1057/9781137406286.0011.

Addressing immoral phlegmatism

Throughout this book I have developed an argument that both individual and organizational attitudes towards fraud in general, but specifically fraud measurement, may be described as *immoral phlegmatism*. To recap, this phenomenon may be defined as an 'anti-moral panic', manifesting itself as a very relaxed, even complacent attitude to all aspects of fraud. The consequence of the phlegmatism, which may be a result of naïvety or self-interest, is an immoral response to fraud in many organizations as well as in state institutions.

This viewpoint is evidenced by some of the explanations offered as to why certain organizations fail to measure fraud. Two in particular worth revisiting are from respondents that evidence this approach is prevalent within the VC sector: the first suggesting that because the organization is a religious charity, there is no fraud and the second advising that fraud measurement is afforded a low priority because the risk is perceived to be low. This suggests a very complacent attitude when a not for profit organization makes such a statement without at least attempting to look for the existence of fraud, particularly when current estimates, which potentially may undercount losses, indicate that fraud costs registered charities £147 million per annum (NFA, 2013, p. 21). Evidence has also been presented of similar attitudes within the public and private sectors, with a local authority fraud manager suggesting that senior management are ambivalent towards fraud and a respondent representing the insurance industry advising that there is little concern that fraud is occurring within the organization.

The survey data reflects that 29 per cent of respondents indicated that their organization failed to measure fraud, offering the explanation that this is because there is no fraud in their organization. This is a somewhat paradoxical situation, because if they do not measure, then how do they know there is no fraud? A further 10 per cent suggested that fraud was not measured because the organization did not need to know, thus evidencing a somewhat naïve attitude towards fraud and its associated risks. Further confirmation of the need for a cultural change is provided by the argument offered against mandating measurement that such exercises may be too costly.

In Chapter 1 the cost of measuring fraud was discussed and arguments presented that this can be a cost-effective process with associated business benefits, these being:

▶ A potential 12:1 return in investment (Gee, 2009a, p. 20).

▸ Regular measurement exercises reduce loss by up to 40 per cent within the first year (Button and Gee, 2013, p. 187).

▸ 'Taken as a proportion of the measured losses, this equates to two per cent being added to the "bottom line" within a year' (Gee, 2010a, p. 13).

▸ Empirical evidence suggests that regular measurement can potentially result in an average increase in profitability of 'almost 36 per cent' (Button and Gee, 2013, p. 187).

Evidence in the form of case studies has also been presented, supporting the argument that the costs of regular fraud loss measurement exercises can be offset by the savings resulting from informed use of the resultant data to develop control strategies, implement focused deployment of any investigative resource and undertake recovery action of identified losses. To summarize, the following case studies evidence the cost effectiveness of regular fraud loss measurement exercises:

▸ 'As a result of IPIA, by the end of FY 2012, the US Administration avoided $50 billion in improper payments' (Payment Accuracy, n.d.).

▸ In FY 2011 over $4 billion dollars of improper payments were recovered, which represents 'the single largest health care fraud recovery in history' (US Energy and Commerce Committee Subcommittee on Health, 2012, p. 1).

▸ The NHS, which had a budget of £87.2 billion for 2005/2006, reduced losses by up to 60 per cent during the period 1998 and 2006 (National Health Service Counter Fraud and Security Management Service, 2007).

▸ The US Department of Agriculture reduced losses by 28 per cent within a £12 billion dollar program between 2002 and 2004 (United States Department of Agriculture, 2002, 2003, 2004).

▸ The Department for Work and Pensions reduced losses in the two means tested benefits Income Support and Jobseekers Allowance that have an annual expenditure of £11.4 billion by 50 per cent between 1997/1998 and 2005/2006 (Department for Work and Pensions, 2007).

To address this mindset, it is imperative that there is a cultural shift towards embracing the value of measurement, so that any form of mandating would be met with less resistance due to organizations having been educated in the financial benefits of accurate fraud measurement.

DOI: 10.1057/9781137406286.0011

This strategy can be progressed by a marketing campaign that delivers awareness training about both organizational vulnerability to fraud, and a positive message about the benefits of proactive fraud loss measurement. In support of the latter argument, I proffer the view of one respondent who suggested the need for a cultural change to make fraud measurement a positive experience. This is a valid point, and can be achieved by emphasizing the business benefits in terms of stemming losses through regular measurement. Equally, the proposed marketing campaign should incorporate the message that there is no organizational stigma attached to being the victim of a fraudulent attack. The issue, however, is that the message needs to emphasize that acknowledging the existence of fraud is not injurious, but failing to measure it and then implementing counter-strategies is.

Within the private sector there may be a concern that an admission of the existence of fraud may be counterproductive to the business through adverse publicity. However, more adverse publicity would result from being identified as an organization that is aware of the presence of fraud, but continues to be in denial, or just blatantly refuses to implement fraud loss measurement exercises. Where these complacent attitudes are identified, the solutions should be persuasively emphasized to eradicate *immoral phlegmatism*.

This strategy requires government support, which may take some lobbying due to the costs involved. One option might be for the Cabinet Office to undertake this role. It could take the form of an electronic campaign by email, direct 'mail shots' to organizations or even newspaper and television advertisements. However, a more suitable alternative would be for the government to task an academic institution specializing in counter-fraud studies to undertake this marketing campaign. This option could improve the potential for cooperation, because any message coming from academia may be seen as being impartial. Furthermore, subject to funding, this academic institution could also be given the remit of continuing the Annual Fraud Indicator, which is a function of the NFA that has not been redistributed following the government announcement that it is to be abolished.

There is also a need for supplementary research within the VC sector on awareness of, and attitudes towards fraud, with a view to developing a marketing strategy to develop a better understanding of vulnerability to fraud within this sector. The research conducted by the Fraud Advisory Panel (2009) into fraud within this sector offers a model that can be used

DOI: 10.1057/9781137406286.0011

as a starting point to inform and direct the proposed research project. This research would enable a strategy to be developed to increase fraud awareness, reduce *immoral phlegmatism* within this sector, and more importantly, incentivize these organizations to measure so that losses can be reduced and more help given to those in need.

Defining fraud for measurement purposes

To achieve a more accurate fraud measure, a standard definition of fraud for this specific purpose is necessary. This will restrict individual interpretation and provide all organizations with a common starting point. When developing a standard definition, this must be suitable for all sectors, and one which may be applied to any unit within the statistically valid sample. This definition should be legally based to prevent any inconsistency in measures, thus removing any doubts on the reliability of data outputs. While the Fraud Act 2006 is informative, this statute is not considered suitable for the purposes of measurement because it only provides definitions of how fraud may be perpetrated.

When developing such a classification, the civil definition *Derry v Peek* (1889) is also worthy of consideration because it is based upon the balance of probabilities, which offers a less stringent test than criminal law. This concept of civil fraud occurs where *someone knowingly or recklessly obtains resources to which they are not entitled*. An alternative option considered was the Audit Commission (2013, p. 8) definition of fraud, which encompasses both internal and external fraud, defining it as 'any intentional false representation, including failure to declare information or abuse of position which is carried out to make gain or cause loss or such as disciplinary action has been taken'.

Both of the aforementioned are suitable because they offer a conceptual definition rather than focusing on enforcement. This is important because it enables any measurement decision-making process to be based upon the balance of probabilities, rather than the criminal law requirement of beyond reasonable doubt. Applying one of these definitions for the purpose of fraud measurement would enable the calculation of a more realistic loss figure. I have previously argued against fraud measurement being based upon detected cases, because lack of evidence to support a criminal sanction would result in these being discounted, even though there may be a strong suspicion of fraud. Furthermore, from

DOI: 10.1057/9781137406286.0011

inception, 'fraud takes 3.4 years to detect' (KPMG, 2011, p. 6), therefore solely relying on detected fraud would further increase the inaccuracy of any loss data. Since the proposed definition needs to be legally based, I advocate that the accepted civil definition of fraud *Derry v Peek* (1889) should be adopted as a standard definition for fraud loss measurement purposes. This could then form the basis for developing an international standard of measurement.

Who should measure?

Subject to statistical validation through the creation of a British Standard of measurement, with the exception of any *Annual Fraud Indicator*, 'hybrid' style fraud loss data measurement reporting should be discontinued. Each organization should be responsible for its own individual loss measurement exercises, conducted to a prescribed standard, and the resultant data be subjected to validation by a mutually appointed third party on a random sample basis. This validator could be an impartial auditor appointed by the organization charged with developing the proposed information exchange and doctrine. These validated data should then be submitted to the organization (academic institution/ private sector partnership) charged with the continuing development and production of the *Annual Fraud Indicator*. I accept that this research has been critical of what have been defined as hybrid reports; however I maintain that the way forward is the construction of an amalgam of fraud loss data, providing that there is consistency of methodology applied in all measurement exercises.

Increasing measurement consistently

There is a need for increased fraud loss measurement. First, because there are organizations from all three sectors represented who fail to measure fraud. I accept that this may be an organizational decision, based on the perception that no fraud exists; however evidence has been presented within this book that when conducting a fraud loss measurement exercise for the first time 'fraud losses will be in the region of 5.7 per cent' (Button and Gee, 2013, p. 75). When examining responses from representatives of organizations across all three sectors, 34 per cent indicated that no fraud measurement took place. The sector which requires most attention however is the VC sector, where responses indicate that 57 per cent of organizations represented failed to carry out any measurement exercises whatsoever. Nevertheless, this is a problem that needs addressing within all sectors, but particularly within charities.

Finally, it is worth considering opinion on the frequency of measurement. While 74 per cent of respondents indicated annually, this still leaves 26 per cent who do not consider this is ideal. Interestingly, some responses suggested that annually it is too infrequent, but realistically it is not cost effective, or of value to measure fraud too frequently because the impact of changes to counter-strategies on losses takes time to evidence.

When advocating increased measurement, this should be directed towards organizations that fail to measure, and those that measure less frequently than annually. There must be a consistent frequency of measurement, which should be annually, and be prescribed within the proposed British Standard of fraud measurement. By adopting this policy, while it may be seen as no change by those already measuring annually, overall it would result in increased fraud loss measurement exercises, which in turn would generate a more accurate calculation of overall losses.

Mandating measurement

Survey data when extrapolated to sector level reveal that within organizations represented within the sample, fraud is not measured by 30 per cent (public), 28 per cent (private) and 57 per cent (VC). Should those responses reflect the attitude to fraud of the wider population, then I contend these data support the argument presented for mandating the measurement of fraud. Responses also evidence that there is no measurement within some local and central government departments and certain organizations within the private sector industries of insurance, retail and manufacturing. The survey also suggests there is some support within organizations for a stronger focus on measurement; however this may be only achieved through some form of mandating. I argue this because while survey respondents answered favourably to this question, this stance may not be representative of all senior influential decision makers within the organization.

DOI: 10.1057/9781137406286.0011

Having considered views on the general mandating of fraud measurement, this research then evaluated reaction to the principle research argument proposing legislation mandating the measurement of fraud. The survey participants indicated significant support for creating a statute, with 76 per cent being in favour. There are also encouraging levels of support from both fraud professionals and academics interviewed; however there is some division between support for developing a more accurate measure across all three sectors and creating a statute-mandating fraud measurement within all three sectors. I have therefore initially considered the option of persuasion as an alternative to regulation.

The art of persuasion

According to Braithwaite (2006b, p. 886) 'law enforcers should be responsive to how effectively … corporations are regulating themselves before deciding whether to escalate intervention'. I have therefore explored whether persuasive tactics could be used to encourage the development of a more accurate measure of fraud. First, when considering the public sector, this has already been attempted by HM Treasury within central government, but with very limited success. A more recent development has been the creation of the Cabinet Office's FED Taskforce which aims to 'reduce the impact of fraud and error' within the entire public sector (Her Majesty's Government, 2012, p. 6). While the Cabinet Office may have some authority, they have not been given sufficient power to compel the public sector to conduct fraud loss measurement exercises and are only able to offer incentives to measure. Consequently, even persuasive directives may not fully address the limited activity within central and local government. Furthermore, when attempting to influence the public sector to measure fraud, the FED Taskforce are still advocating the measurement of fraud by examining detected cases rather than compelling central government departments to undertake proactive fraud loss risk measurement exercises (Her Majesty's Government, 2012, p. 17).

Equally, the first FED Taskforce publication which discusses areas of priority including 'the independent assessment of the accuracy of estimated and reported losses' only makes reference to the consistent estimate of 'spend metrics' (Cabinet Office, 2011, p. 14). While this criterion is important, the fact that there is no reference to consistent fraud loss measurement gives cause for concern that inconsistencies in fraud loss measurement, including what is counted and the methodology employed, will remain within this sector.

Finally, I return to the empirical evidence offered by the US example, whereby failed attempts at persuasion the US government necessitated the creation of the IPIA of 2002 which requires public agencies to publish statistically valid estimates of the levels of fraud within their programs and activities. I therefore suggest that persuasion is not an option for the UK public sector and regulation through intervention is the only viable option to obtain consistently accurate fraud loss data.

Moving on to consider the private sector, there is evidence that fraud loss measurement takes place; however this activity does not always take place on a consistent basis, as evidenced within the last Annual Fraud Indicator which contains data for the latest year that figures are available, ranging from 2006 to 2013 (NFA, 2013, p. 4). This suggests that despite the efforts of the NFA, there are still private sector organizations that cannot be persuaded to supply extant data or fail to measure regularly. In fact, representatives from this sector have actually admitted at the regional NFA fraud summits (NFA, 2009) that this is the case, whereby certain industries stated that they will only provide fraud loss data if compelled to do so by their regulator or by legislation.

Evidence is contained within from the NFA's *Annual Fraud Indicator* of reluctance to provide fraud loss data. The 2011 private sector fraud loss estimate (excluding financial and insurance industries) was obtained through an online questionnaire. Respondents were asked to provide an estimate of fraud against their organization as a percentage of annual turnover; however 'almost half of respondents chose the option "prefer not to say"' (NFA, 2012, p. 16). Furthermore, the NFA (2012, p. 6) acknowledge limitations in the private sector fraud loss data resulting from 'the potential bias of organizations self-selecting to participate', which also suggests that persuasion is not a viable option. The findings from the 2012 qualitative survey also reveal limited knowledge about the extent of fraud losses, with many organizations suggesting that it was 'too difficult to place a precise figure on an activity they did not know about' (NFA, 2013, p. 20).

Focusing on the financial services industry, I suggest that the reluctance to supply current and accurate mortgage fraud data also evidences that persuasive tactics have not worked. Accordingly, the estimate for mortgage fraud is given a poor level of confidence by the NFA and the figure has not actually changed since 2009 (NFA, 2013, p. 42). Therefore, to develop a

DOI: 10.1057/9781137406286.0011

more accurate measure of fraud, state intervention as opposed to persuasion may be the only viable option, as evidenced by the necessity for the state to intervene during the banking crisis resulting from irresponsible practices, and the subsequent regulation imposed to control the future activities of these institutions. Of equal concern is the fraud loss data supplied by the insurance industry, which is only given an average confidence rating (NFA, 2013, p. 39). This is because the industry only supplies partial fraud loss data for the general insurance market and excludes the long-term market. Again this suggests there may be a need to consider alternatives to persuasion to obtain full and accurate fraud loss data.

Finally, I return to the Bribery Act 2010 which I suggest offers empirical evidence that private sector organizations may only comply with government-imposed procedures through regulation. This statute imposes a legal requirement for the implementation of internal processes at a cost to the organization to limit the risks of bribery taking place. Therefore if the state needs to intervene to ensure that profit-making organizations put costly measures in place to remove the risk of bribery, then why not for fraud losses which reduce profitability?

Moving on to consider the VC sector, it is imperative that this sector further develop an understanding of fraud, but most importantly, acknowledge the importance of accurate measurement. Since this sector is still in the early stages of embracing the concept of fraud measurement, there is scope to persuade not for profit organizations to implement fraud loss measurement programs without resorting to mandating the process. Furthermore, regulating this sector may be viewed as too draconian, and thus creates resistance to any proposed statute, which may not be so vehement should they be excluded.

To emphasize the importance of fraud loss measurement, and as a consequence, to improve the quality of loss data from this sector, the government could task a specialist accounting firm, for example BDO, to conduct fraud measurement exercises within a sample of VC sector organizations. While the identity of the organizations involved would remain anonymous, the results of the exercise could be circulated to the 1,599 charities with an income in excess of £100,000 (NFA, 2013, p. 8). Should the results of these exercises indicate the prevalence of fraud as research suggests, sight of these data will incentivize other charitable organizations to measure.

Furthermore, to improve the accuracy of VC sector loss data, organizations with a minimum turnover of £10 million could be persuaded to conduct measurement exercises on a voluntary basis, with a 95 per cent level of statistical confidence but a less stringent accuracy level of +/-2.5 per cent, but with the aim of gradually improving accuracy levels to those within the proposed British Standard of Measurement. A small sample of these proposed voluntary loss measurement exercises could be independently validated, and these figures extrapolated to provide a more realistic estimation of fraud losses throughout the VC sector. Once the benefits of regular loss measurement are evidenced by those organizations participating, this should persuade more charities to conduct fraud loss measurement exercises, thus further improving data accuracy. Until business savings are evidenced, this could be achieved by offering incentives to persuade charitable organizations that they need to measure fraud. These might include:

▸ increasing the value of 'gift aid' that charities claim back from the government,
▸ no business tax,
▸ free advertising via government networks to generate additional donations.

Creating a statute

Having discounted the option that the public and private sectors can be persuaded to measure fraud accurately and consistently, this book proposes that a statute similar to the US IPIA 2002 should be created. The legislation should incorporate the proposed British Standard of Measurement, thus ensuring consistency of data accuracy, and stipulate that all organizations encapsulated by this statute apply the model. Without such a standard to accompany the proposed regulation, there would be no guarantee of data consistency. Initially, such legislation should be directed towards the public sector at central and local government levels and large private sector organizations.

When considering which private sector organizations should be included in the proposed statute, one option is to include all those with shareholders, thus incorporating public limited companies, private limited companies and private unlimited companies. The legislation could then offer shareholders a vote on whether the business should comply, but with a caveat that should they vote against, they must inform the regulating authority and details of organizations failing to comply

DOI: 10.1057/9781137406286.0011

following a shareholder vote are made public. However, this option has been discounted because it takes no account of company size and therefore might include businesses without the capacity to fulfil their obligations.

I therefore advocate inclusion of all private sector organizations excluding those classed as small- and medium-sized enterprises (European Commission, 2005), because they may have problems self-regulating in any form (Aalders and Wilthagan, 1997; Ayres and Braithwaite, 1992, p. 121) due to limited capacity. The inclusion criteria for the proposed statute are therefore all private sector organizations with a minimum headcount of 250 and whose annual turnover is $\geq €50$ million (sterling equivalent) or annual balance sheet is $\geq €43$ (sterling equivalent) (European Commission, 2005).

The Cabinet Office, or alternatively an independent organization, could be charged with overseeing the regulation of the statute and funded accordingly. While it may be suggested that any savings generated by these proposed exercises will only benefit a commercially driven enterprise, it is worth remembering that certain organizations pass on fraud losses to their customers. Therefore, a reduction in these losses resulting in increased profits could potentially benefit the consumer should these organizations be persuaded to pass on some of these savings, for example in the form of reduced insurance premiums or bank charges. Secondly, the financial benefits of reducing fraud losses could also have a positive impact on the UK economy due to the anticipated increase in consumer disposable income and increased company profits which could result in expansion, more employment opportunities and increased contributions to HM Treasury through taxes.

To facilitate the proposed regulatory model, a state-funded fraud loss measurement training program delivered on behalf of the Cabinet Office could be offered to ensure that those businesses without the expertise can recruit and train staff in fraud loss measurement in preparation for the commencement of enforced self-regulation. The additional costs can be met from the potential savings achieved from eliminating the vulnerabilities identified once fraud loss measurement exercises commence. The probable increase in company profits and the resultant increased revenue to the treasury are offered as justification for this proposed state-funded intervention.

The potential resistance from the private sector to publishing these data has been considered; I accept that as a commercial organization, representatives of the private sector may be reluctant to comply. To reach a compromise, it is suggested that private sector organizations impacted upon by this legislation demonstrate that they have complied with their statutory obligations, and offer their data for independent scrutiny on a random sampling basis. This would prevent private sector organizations citing commercial self-interest as an argument against the creation of such a statute. To facilitate this proposal, I advocate the creation of a government-funded validation team that examines methodology and signs off any data as being statically valid in accordance with the statute, and produces a certificate of compliance which evidences that fraud has been measured in accordance with proposed standards. These data would then be submitted to whoever takes over responsibility for the Annual Fraud Indicator for inclusion, but remain 'commercial in confidence' and only incorporated into the industry-specific loss calculation.

Any costs incurred will be offset by potential savings, and should certainly be factored into any public sector departmental business plan. In terms of the private sector, these mandating proposals may actually have a positive effect on the economy, by reducing business losses and increasing profitability. Once a British Standard has been created, private sector accounting and auditing organizations could in fact generate income by offering their services as a peripatetic measurement team to private and VC sector organizations that may prefer to invest in an external service rather than employ permanent measurement staff. Any organization undertaking this function would of course need to prove itself as competent, by evidencing compliance with the British Standard, and undergo periodic auditing to ensure consistency.

Regulating the sectors

Public sector

Regulation is defined as a 'means to control or direct others by rules, standards or principles' (Braithwaite, 2006a, p. 1). Regulating the public sector poses less of a problem than the private sector because the core executive which includes that Treasury and the Cabinet Office has a range of 'rule-making powers' (James, 2005, p. 326) to facilitate implementation and seek compliance. Furthermore, the IPIA provides a working model which can be used to inform the development of the regulatory process of the proposed statute. The implementation of IPIA by public sector

DOI: 10.1057/9781137406286.0011

bodies relies upon independent regulation from within, whereby each Federal Agency conducts loss measurement exercises and reports their findings to the OMB via the Agency's Performance and Accountability Report or Annual Financial Report. In terms of auditing, each agency's Inspector General reviews the organization's improper payment reporting and accompanying materials to ensure compliance with IPIA.

The regulatory model proposed for ensuring public sector compliance with the proposed UK statute is drawn from the US. Each public sector body will be made responsible for conducting fraud loss measurement exercises and reporting findings direct to the Cabinet Office, or the organization charged with producing an Annual Fraud Indicator. The auditing of central government fraud loss measurement reporting is allocated to the National Audit Office (NAO), and that of local government and other public sector bodies such as NHS trusts conducted by the Audit Commission and transferred to the NAO following implementation of the proposed closure of the former.

To supplement this process, consideration has been given to the imposition of sanctions for non-compliance. It is important that these are similar in terms of impact to those applied to the private sector to maintain equality and remove the risk of allegations of unfair treatment. The first stage therefore is a letter to the departmental head advocating implementation of the required measurement program within six months. Failure to comply will result in a referral to the Committee of Public Accounts who will seek an explanation from the head of department, with the resultant penalty for consistent failure to comply being public disclosure of this material fact. By allowing public scrutiny, organizations may be persuaded to comply rather than to risk the possibility of adverse publicity and backlash from taxpayers. The sanction for a second offence would be linked to budgets because central government departments are allocated funding based upon performance in the previous two years. Failure to comply would result in a funding freeze until the department has demonstrated compliance. The potential threat of funding being capped at existing levels should be sufficient motivation for organizational heads to comply.

Private sector

When regulating the private sector I propose an enforced self-regulatory model whereby the government writes the rules defining the measurement

DOI: 10.1057/9781137406286.0011

process to be followed. This will assist companies that do not have sufficient expertise to write their own processes. Each individual business then selects all appropriate specified transactions and performs fraud loss measurement exercises using their own staff, and appoints an internal compliance group who audit and issue a certificate of compliance. The government also appoints a team of inspectors who conduct random audits of companies. Embracing the spirit of market testing, this function could be performed by a contracted private sector accounting company which is overseen by the Cabinet Office. Any unacceptable accounting practices within the measurement exercises identified by the independent auditors would constitute a violation of the regulations and the appropriate sanction applied. All fraud loss measurement data are sent to the organization charged with producing the *Annual Fraud Indicator* but individual organizational data are not released into the public domain. The advantages of this model are that it is easier and more efficient to perform than direct government regulation and enables simplified comparable accounting.

Successful regulation necessitates a balance being struck between punitiveness and persuasion (Ayres and Braithwaite, 1992, p. 25). When considering the appropriate punishment I propose a sequence of sanctions based on the lower half of the regulatory enforcement pyramid (Braithwaite, 2002, p. 20) that provides the options of persuasion, warning letter and civil penalty. In terms of non-compliance, one essential component of the IPIA 2002 is that details of all organizations that fail to comply are made public. This is a deterrent option that should be incorporated into the proposed statute. The first stage of the process would be a letter advising the business that they have a set period to comply, and should they fail to do so, their details will be included on a list of 'non-compliers' published on the Cabinet Office website and launched by a press release.

Setting a standard

To support the mandating of fraud there is a requirement for a prescriptive standard of how fraud should be measured which includes direction on the following:

▸ sampling criteria
▸ the level of statistical confidence to ensure consistent high standards of accuracy

DOI: 10.1057/9781137406286.0011

▶ what is measured, thus providing consistency of data and enabling comparability by sector, industry and fraud typology
▶ the frequency of these measurement exercises.

Compliance with these instructions should be mandatory, which can be achieved by incorporating the proposed standard into the previously discussed statute. Government departments that already have prescribed measurement methodology such as DWP and HMRC will be required to amend their processes accordingly. This standard, once established, should form the basis for the future development of an international standard, which would then facilitate transnational comparability.

It is crucial that any standard should stipulate what is measured and the methodology employed. I therefore recommend the proposed standard should incorporate the following:

▶ Measurement should only include fraud and exclude losses resulting from error.
▶ All internal and external fraud losses are measured.
▶ Guidance should be proffered on what typologies should be measured including customer fraud, procurement fraud, payroll fraud, expenses/subsistence fraud, major company expenditure. This would enable cross-sector comparative analysis by typology.
▶ All loss measurement exercises should focus on the risk of losses and not just reported or detected fraud.
▶ The accuracy level of the common sample should be ±1 per cent with 95 per cent statistical confidence for all government departments and large private sector organizations.
▶ Due to cost implications, an alternative option is offered to private sector organizations which evidence inadequate financial capacity to apply the higher accuracy standard. The proposed alternative being an accuracy level of ±2.5 per cent with 90 per cent statistical confidence, but with a prescribed timescale to move to the higher accuracy standard.
▶ The measurement methodology should employ statistically valid sampling, with the results being extrapolated to reflect the total extent of estimated losses.
▶ Measurement exercises should be based upon a standard definition of fraud for this purpose, underpinned by a 'balance of probabilities' determination (Derry v Peek 1889) which offers better recovery options, thus contributing to the cost effectiveness of the exercise.

▶ All exercises should be subjected to independent scrutiny and validation to ensure accuracy, probity and transparency.

▶ Where private sector organizations do not publish their fraud loss data, following validation, a certificate of compliance is issued to evidence that losses have been measured to the prescribed standard.

Knowledge management

To improve the quality and robustness of fraud loss data collection and reporting, there is also an urgent need for an academic steer on developing doctrine. This input would raise the level of measurement expertise and improve the quality of reporting by offering guidance on writing reports that stand up to academic scrutiny. To achieve openness and transparency, they should include a discussion of the data collection methodology, details of the analytical process these data were subjected to, frankness in disclosing any data limitations and a clear and concise written style which presents the facts in a medium that can be understood by fraud professionals, strategists and policy makers.

To achieve this, I advocate a knowledge management infrastructure to ensure compliance with the recommended British Standard of measurement. This proposed conduit would take the form of regular three monthly meetings, populated with fraud measurement practitioners from all three sectors. The primary focus of this forum would be to discuss best practice, share experiences and disclose any new and innovative processes adopted which have improved the accuracy of measurement, or acted as an enabler to ensure compliance with the proposed British Standard. By regularly reviewing processes, empirical learning can be used to create a Manual of Guidance to support compliance with the British Standard. Furthermore, this proposed manual will be 'owned' by this forum and updated as and when there are positive developments in measurement processes.

It is vital that this proposed knowledge management infrastructure is seen to be neutral, and should therefore be overseen by an appropriate organization. The most feasible option for this proposal might be a forum that is sponsored and funded by government, but managed and overseen by an academic institution. This would ensure probity, facilitate the unification of practitioners and academics when developing best

DOI: 10.1057/9781137406286.0011

practice and ensure theoretical and practice-based input into the creation of any 'manual of guidance'.

Review

This chapter has outlined the recommendations of this research project. I maintain that sufficient opinion has been collected to evaluate the viability of the research argument, and sufficient encouragement from respondents has been harvested to support the contention that the proposals outlined within this chapter are worthy of development collectively.

The data limitations in terms of generalizability have been acknowledged; however I contend that the support proffered for the proposals may be considered to be a barometer of a wider population. In summary, this book concludes that the creation of a statute-mandating fraud measurement, incorporating a British Standard underpinned by a universal definition of fraud for measurement purposes, are worthy of development. Therefore, the next step will be to identify an appropriate government minister and lobby support for these proposals. Additionally, this project has evidenced the requirement to establish a knowledge management infrastructure to support the implementation of the aforementioned proposals through the development of core doctrine of measurement and the production of a manual of guidance. I consider the most suitable organization to facilitate such a forum to be an academic institution, thus ensuring impartiality and probity.

The research has also identified the phenomena of *immoral phlegmatism* within all three sectors, which manifests itself in the form of complacency towards vulnerability to fraud and resultant losses. The data garnered however suggests that it is most prevalent within the VC sector, and strategies have been proposed to bring about a sea change of attitude towards fraud losses. In terms of this sector, I have also recommended that further research is conducted into why there is such a complacent attitude to fraud, which in turn would inform the proposed awareness strategy discussed in this chapter.

Finally, during the course of writing this book the closure of the NFA was announced, and as yet, production of the Annual Fraud Indicator has not been redistributed. The purpose of the recommendations of this research is to produce a more accurate measure of fraud that can be released into the public domain. Accordingly, it is imperative that the Annual Fraud Indicator continues. This book therefore recommends that the government sponsors the continued publication of an indicator, which could be produced by an academic institution in partnership with a private sector accounting organization. This partnership could coordinate the collection, auditing and publication of loss data following the creation of legislation mandating the measurement of fraud.

DOI: 10.1057/9781137406286.0011

References

Aalders, M. and Wilthagan, T. (1997) 'Moving Beyond Command and Control: Reflexivity in the Regulation of Occupational Safety and Health', *Law and Policy*, 19(4), 415–443.

Aaronovitch, S. (1983) 'A Marxist View', in M. Friedman, M. Peston, S. Aaronovitch, A. Singh and I. Bruegel (eds), *Money Talks: Five Views of Britain's Economy* (London: Thames Television International), pp. 34–53.

Adams, I. (2001) *Political Ideology Today*, 2nd edn (Manchester: Manchester University Press).

Allen, J., Forrest, S., Levi, M., Roy, H., Sutton, M. and Wilson, D. (2005) *Fraud and Technology Crimes: Findings from the2002/03 British Crime Survey and 2003 Offending, Crime and Justice Survey* (London: Home Office).

Alvarez, A. (2010) *Genocidal Crimes* (Abingdon: Routledge).

Ambler, D. E., Massaro, L. and Acre, J. W. (2010) *Sarbanes Oxley Act: Planning and Compliance* (New York: Aspen Publishers).

Amin, S. and Chaudhury, N. (2008) 'An Introduction to Methodologies for Measuring Service Delivery in Education', in S. Amin, J. Das and M. Goldstein (eds) *Are You Being Served? New Tools for Measuring Service Delivery* (Washington, DC: World Bank), pp. 67–110.

Anderson, S. and Heywood, P. M. (2009) 'The Politics of Perception: Use and Abuse of Transparency International's Approach to Measuring Corruption', *Political Studies*, 57, 746–767.

DOI: 10.1057/9781137406286.0012

Arrow, K. J. (1978) 'Foreword', in B. A. Weisbrod, J. F. Handler and N. K. Komesar (eds), *Public Interest Law: An Economic and Institutional Analysis* (Los Angeles, CA: University of California Press), pp. ix–x.

Association for Payment Clearing Services (2009) *Fraud: The Facts 2009* (London: APACS).

Association of British Insurers (2009) *General Insurance Claims Fraud Research Brief*, July (London: Association of British Insurers).

Audit Commission (2009) *Protecting the Public Purse* (London: Audit Commission).

Audit Commission (2010) *Protecting the Public Purse* (London: Audit Commission).

Audit Commission (2011) *Protecting the Public Purse* (London: Audit Commission).

Audit Commission (2013) *Protecting the Public Purse* (London: Audit Commission).

Auditing Practices Board (2010) International Standard on Auditing (UK and Ireland 240), http://www.frc.org.uk/FRC-Documents/APB/ The-auditor-s-responsibilities-relating-to-fraud-i.aspx, date accessed 21 April 2013.

Ayres, I. and Braithwaite, J. (1992) *Responsive Regulation: Transcending the Deregulation Debate* (New York: Oxford University Press).

BDO (2010) *FRAUDTRACK 7: Perspectives of Fraud* (Leeds: BDO).

BDO (2014) *BDO Fraudtrack Report Reveals Sharp Increase in Money Laundering in the UK*, http://www.bdo.co.uk/press/bdo-fraudtrack-report-reveals-sharp-increase-in-money-laundering-in-the-uk, date accessed 04 February 2014.

Belli, P. (1997) *The Comparative Advantage of Government: A Review*, Policy Research Working Paper 1834 (Washington, DC: World Bank).

Benefit Fraud Inspectorate (1998) *Securing the System: A Report by the Director General* (London: Department of Social Security).

Bitner, R. (2008) *Greed, Fraud and Ignorance: A Subprime Insider's Look at the Mortgage Collapse* (Colleyville, Texas: LTV Media LLC).

Blunt, G. and Hand, D. J. (2007) *Estimating the Iceberg: How Much Fraud is there in the UK?* http://qfrmc.imaa.ic.ac.uk/qfrmc/23nov07/talks/ gordon/.pdf, date accessed 16 December 2008.

Braithwaite, J. (1985) *To Punish or Persuade: Enforcement of Coal Mine Safety* (Albany, NY: State University of New York Press).

Braithwaite, J. (2002) 'Rewards and Regulation', *Journal of Law and Society*, 29(1), 12–26.

DOI: 10.1057/9781137406286.0012

Braithwaite, J. (2006b) 'Responsive Regulation and Developing Economies', *World Development*, 34(5), 884–898.

Braithwaite, V. (2006a) Ten Things you Need to Know about Regulation but Never Wanted to Ask. *Regulatory Institutions Network, Occasional Paper No 8*, December 2006.

Brand, S. and Price, R. (2000) *The Economic and Social Costs of Crime*, Home Office Research Study 217 (London: Home Office).

British Broadcasting Corporation (2009) *Recession Fuels Insurance Fraud*, http://news.bbc.co.uk/1/hi/business/8000630.stm, date accessed 11 August 2010.

British Retail Consortium (2009) *Retail Crime Survey 2009* (London: British Retail Consortium).

British Standards Institute (2000) *A Guide to the Application of Statistical Methods to Quality and Standardization*, BS 600:2000 (London: British Standards Institute).

British Standards Institute (2002) *Sampling Procedures for Inspection by Attributes–Part 5: Procedures foe assessment of Declared Quality Levels*, BS6001–5:2002 (London: British Standards Institute).

British Standards Institute Case Study (n.d.) *BSI 10500 Case Study: Specification for an Anti–Bribery Management System*, http://www.bsigroup.co.uk/Documents/bs-10500/resources/case%20studies/BSI-BS10500-Case-Study-BalfourBeatty-UK-EN.pdf, date accessed 10 May 2013.

Brooks, G., Button, M. and Frimpong, K. (2009) 'Policing Fraud in the Private Sector: A Survey of the FTSE 100 Companies in the UK', *International Journal of Police Science and Management*, 11(4), 493–504.

Button, M. and Gee, J. (2013) *Countering Fraud for Competitive Advantage: The Professional Approach to Reducing the Last Great Hidden Cost* (Chichester: John Wiley).

Budd, T., Sharp, C. and Mayhew, P. (2005) *Offending in England and Wales: First Results from the 2003 Crime and Justice Survey*, Research Study No. 275 (London: Home Office).

Button, M., Gee, J. and Brooks, G. (2012) 'Measuring the Cost of Fraud: An Opportunity for the New Competitive Advantage', *Journal of Financial Crime*, 19(1), 65–75.

Button, M., Johnston, L. and Frimpong, K. (2008) 'The Fraud Review and the Policing of Fraud: Laying the Foundations for a centralized Fraud Police or Counter Fraud Executive?' *Policing*, 2(2), 241–250.

Button, M. and Tunley, M. (2014) *Explaining Fraud Deviancy Attenuation* (Unpublished Paper).

Cabinet Office (2011) *Eliminating Public Sector Fraud: The Counter Fraud Taskforce Interim Report* (London: Cabinet Office).

Cardilli, M. C. (2003) 'Regulation Without Borders: The Impact of Sarbanes–Oxley on European Companies', *Fordham International Law Journal*, 27(2), 785–822.

Channel Four News (2009) *FactCheck: Bailout Spin?*, http://www.channel4.com/news/articles/business_money/factcheck+bailout+spin/290, date accessed 21 July 2010.

CIFAS (2011) *Fraudscape: Depicting the UK's Fraud Landscape* (London: CIFAS).

CIFAS (2012) *Fraudscape: Depicting the UK's Fraud Landscape*, https://www.cifas.org.uk/secure/contentPORT/uploads/documents/reports/Confidential-%20Fraudscape%202011.pdf, date accessed 12 July 2012.

CIFAS (2013) *Fraudscape: Depicting the UK's Fraud Landscape*, https://www.cifas.org.uk/secure/contentPORT/uploads/documents/CIFAS%20Reports/External-Fraudscape_2013_CIFAS.pdf, date accessed 05 February 2014.

Cohen, S. (1972) *Folk Devils and Moral Panics: The Creation of the Mods and Rockers* (London: MacGibbon and Kee).

Cohen, S. (1980) *Folk Devils and Moral Panics*, 2nd edn (London: Martin Robertson).

Cohen, S. (2002) *Folk Devils and Moral Panics*, 30th anniversary edn (London: Routledge).

Coleman, C. and Moynihan, J. (1996) *Understanding Crime Data: Haunted by the Dark Figure* (Buckingham: Open University Press).

Cullinan, C. (2004) 'Enron as a Symptom of Audit Process Breakdown: Can the Sarbanes–Oxley Act Cure the Disease?', *Critical Perspectives on Accounting*, 15, 853–864.

Daily Telegraph (2009) *IMF Puts Total Cost of Crisis at £7.1 Trillion.*, http://www.telegraph.co.uk/finance/newsbysector/banksandfinance/5995810/IMF-puts-total-cost-of-crisis-at-7.1-trillion.html, date accessed 15 December 2009.

Denscombe, M. (2010) *The Good Research Guide: For Small Scale Social Research Projects,* 4th edn (Maidenhead: Open University Press).

Department for Work and Pensions (2005) *Fraud Error and Other Incorrectness in Disability Living Allowance* (London: DWP).

DOI: 10.1057/9781137406286.0012

Department for Work and Pensions (2007) *Fraud and Error in the Benefits System April 2005 to March 2006* (London: DWP).

Department for Work and Pensions (2008) *Fraud and Error in the Benefits System: April 2007 to March 2008* (London: DWP).

Department for Work and Pensions (2013) *Fraud and Error in the Benefits System: Preliminary 2012/13 Estimates (Great Britain)* (Newcastle: DWP).

Doig, A. (2006) *Fraud* (Cullompton: Willan).

Doig, A., Johnson, S. and Levi, M. (2001) 'New Public Management, Old Populism and the Policing of Fraud', *Public Policy and Administration*, 16(1), 91–113.

Doig, A. and Levi, M. (2009) 'Inter–agency Work and the UK Public Sector Investigation of Fraud 1996–2006: Joined up Rhetoric and Disjointed Reality', *Policing and Society*, 19(3), 199–215.

Doig, A. and Macaulay, M. (2010) 'Decades, Directions and the Fraud Review: Addressing the Future of Public Sector Fraud?', *Public Money and Management*, 28(3), 185–192.

Driver and Vehicle Licensing Agency (2009) *Annual Report and Accounts* (Swansea: DVLA).

Ernst and Young (2006) *Fraud Risk in Emerging Markets, 9th Global Survey* http://www.ey.com/Global/Assets.nsf/Ireland_EOY_E/ Thought_Leadership_Fraud_Survey/$file/EY_Fraud_Survey_June2006. pdf, date accessed 27 April 2010.

Ernst and Young (2013) *Growing Beyond: A Place for Integrity*, http://www. ey.com/Publication/vwLUAssets/Global-Fraud-Survey -a-place-for-integrity-12th-Global-Fraud-Survey/$FILE/EY-12th-GLOBAL-FRAUD-SURVEY.pdf, date accessed 05 February 2014.

European Commission (2005) *The New SME Definition: User Guide and Model Declaration,* http://ec.europa.eu/enterprise/policies/sme/files/ sme _definition/sme_user_guide_en.pdf, date accessed 25 April 2013.

Fan, S. (2008) *Public Expenditures, Growth and Poverty: Lessons from Developing Countries* (Baltimore, MA: John Hopkins University Press).

Federal Housing Finance Agency Office of Inspector General (2013) *FHFA's Controls to detect and Prevent Improper Payments*, http://fhfaoig. gov/Content /Files/FHFA's%20Controls%20to%20Detect%20and%20 Prevent%20Improper%20Payments.pdf, date accessed 25 April 2013.

Ferguson, N. (2008) *The Ascent of Money: A Financial History of the World* (New York: Penguin).

Financial Fraud Action UK (2013) *Fraud the Facts 2013: The Definitive Overview of Payment Industry Fraud and Measures to Prevent it* (London: Financial Fraud Action UK).

Financial Services Authority (2003). *Developing our Policy on Fraud and Dishonesty*. Discussion Paper 26. London: Financial Services Authority, http://www.fsa.gov.uk/pubs/discussion/dp26.pdf, 19 February 2010.

Fleming, M. (2009) *FSA's Scale and Impact of Financial Crime Project (Phase One): Critical Analysis* (London: The Financial Services Authority).

Foreign and Commonwealth Office (2010) *Resource Accounts 2009–10*, HC74 (London: The Stationery Office).

Foresight Crime Prevention Panel (2006) *Just Around the Corner* (London: Department of Trade and Industry).

Foucault, M. (1977) *Discipline and Punish: The Birth of the Prison* (London: Allen Lane).

Foucault, M. (1979) 'On Governmentality', *Ideology and Consciousness*, 6, 5–22.

Foucault, M. (2000) *Power: Essential Works of Foucault, 1954–1984* (Volume 3), J. D. Faubion (ed.), R. Hurley (Trans.) (London: Penguin Books).

Fraud Advisory Panel (1999) *Studies of Published Literature on the Nature and Extent of Fraud in the Public and Private Sector* (London: Fraud Advisory Panel).

Fraud Advisory Panel (2009) *Fraud in the Charitable Sector* (London: Fraud Advisory Panel).

Fraud Review Team (2006) *Fraud Review: Final Report*: http://www.lslo. gov.uk/pdf/fraudreview.pdf, date accessed 01 August 2006.

Gannon, R. and Doig, A. (2010) 'Ducking the Answer? Fraud Strategies and Police Resources', *Policing and Society*, 20(1), 39–60.

Gee, J. (2007) 'Measuring Fraud' *Fighting Fraud*. Issue 22, 7–9. London: KPMG, http://www.iprisk.co.uk/iprisk2009/documents/ Fighting% 20 Fraud%2022%20FINAL%20web.pdf, date accessed 28 May 2009.

Gee, J. (2009a) 'A New Approach for a New Era', *Fraud Intelligence*, http:// www.fraudeconomics.co.uk/assets/uploads/files/Fraud_Intelligence_-_ Jim_Gee_-_A_New_Approach_for_a_New_Era_-_August_2009.pdf, date accessed 26 April 2010.

Gee, J. (2009b) 'Out of the Ashes', *Public Finance,* November, http:// opinion.publicfinance.co.uk/2009/11/out-of-the-ashes/, date accessed 27 April 2010.

Gee, J. (2010a) 'Fraud: Measure it to Manage it', *International Accountant*, 52, 12–13.

Gee, J. (2010b) 'Bad Medicine', *Public Finance*, January 29–February 4, 24–25.

Gee, J. and Helwig, R. (2008) 'International Healthcare Fraud', *Fighting Fraud*, 25, 18–20, http://www.kpmg.fi/Binary.aspx?Section =174andItem=5241, date accessed 27 April 2010.

Gee, J., Button, M. and Brooks, G. (2009) *The Financial Cost of Fraud* (London: Macintyre Hudson and Portsmouth: University of Portsmouth Centre for Counter Fraud Studies).

Gee, J., Button, M. and Brooks, G. (2010) *The Financial Cost of UK Public Sector Fraud* (Macintyre Hudson: London and University of Portsmouth Centre for Counter Fraud Studies: Portsmouth).

Gordon, G. R. and Willox Jr., N. A. (2005) 'Using Identity Authentication and Eligibility Assessment to Mitigate the Risk of Improper Payment'. *Journal of Economic Crime Management*, 3(1), 1–24.

Gunn, O. (2004) 'Why Do We Have Separate Courses in Macro and Micro and Macro Economics', in E. Fullbrook (ed.) *A Guide to What's Wrong with Economics* (Anthem Press, London).

Gupta, P. P. and Leech, T. (2006) 'Making Sarbanes–Oxley 404 work: Reducing cost, increasing effectiveness', *International Journal of Disclosure and Governance*, 3(1), 27–48.

Hatch, G. and McMurtry, V. A. (2009) *Improper Payments Information Act of 2002: Background, Implementation, and Assessment.* Congressional Research Service, http://assets.opencrs.com/rpts/ RL34164 _20091008.pdf, date accessed 30 July 2010.

Hatch, G. and McMurtry, V. A. (2010) *Improper Payments Information Act of 2002: Background, Implementation, and Assessment.* Congressional Research Service, RL34164, October 04, 2010.Hawken, A. and Munck, L. (2009) *Do You Know Your Data? Measurement Validity in Corruption Research*, http://www.researchgate.net/publication/ 228976780_ Do_you_know_your_data_Measurement_validity _in_corruption_research, date accessed 24 February 2014.

Hellwig, M. (2008) 'Systematic Risk in the Financial Sector: An Analysis of the Sub-prime Mortgage Financial Crisis'. *Preprints of the Max Planck Institute for Research on Collective Goods*, No. 2008, 43.

Hencke, D. and Sparrow, A. (2009) 'Gordon Brown Defends Rescue of Northern Rock after NAO Report', *The Guardian*, http://www.

DOI: 10.1057/9781137406286.0012

guardian.co.uk/ politics/2009/mar/20/northern-rock-mandelson/print, date accessed 21 July 2010.

Her Majesty's Government (2009) *Putting the Frontline First: Smarter Government*. (London: The Stationery Office).

Her Majesty's Government (2012) *Tackling Fraud and Error in Government: A Report of the Fraud, Error and Debt Taskforce* (London: Cabinet Office).

Her Majesty's Revenue and Customs (2006) *Child and Working Tax Credits: Error and Fraud Statistics 2003–04* (London: HMRC).

Her Majesty's Revenue and Customs (2007) *Measuring Indirect Tax Losses – 2007* (London: HMRC).

Her Majesty's Revenue and Customs (2009) *Measuring Tax Gaps 2009* (London: HMRC).

Her Majesty's Revenue and Customs (2013a) *Measuring Tax Gaps 2013 Edition: Tax Gap Estimates for 2011–12* (London: HMRC).

Her Majesty's Revenue and Customs (2013b) *Child and Working Tax Credits: Error and Fraud Statistics 2011–12* (London: HMRC).

Her Majesty's Treasury (1995) *Fraud Report 1994–95* (London: HMSO).

Her Majesty's Treasury (2009a) *2008–2009 Fraud Report: An Analysis of Reported Fraud in Government Departments* (London: Her Majesty's Treasury).

Her Majesty's Treasury (2009b) *Fraud in Government Departments 2009*, Dear Accounting Officer Letter (03/09), http://www.hm-treasury.gov.uk/d/dao0309.pdf 2011, date accessed 23 May 2012.

Higson, A. (1999) *The Fraud Advisory Working Party Paper: Why is Management Reticent to Report Fraud? An Exploratory Study*. https://www.fraudadvisorypanel.org/pdf_show.php?id=28, date accessed 01 May 2013.

Hoare, J. (2007) 'Deceptive Evidence: Challenges in Measuring Fraud', in M. Hough and M. Maxwell (eds), *Surveying Crime in the 21st Century* (Cullompton: Willan), pp. 263–279.

Home Office (2005) *The Economic and Social Costs of Crime Against Individuals and Households 2003–04* (London: Home Office).

Home Office (2013) *Crime Against Businesses: Headline Findings from the 2012 Commercial Victimisation Survey* (London: Home Office).

House of Commons Treasury Committee (2009) *Banking Crisis: Dealing with the Failure of the UK Banks: Government, UK Financial Investments Ltd and Financial Services Authority Responses to the Seventh Report from the Committee.* Seventh Special Report of Session 2008–09. HC956 (London: The Stationery Office).

International Monetary Fund (2000) *World Economic Outlook May 2000: Asset Prices and the Business Cycle* (Washington, DC: International Monetary Fund Publication Services).

James, O. (2005) 'The Rise of Regulation of the Public Sector in the United Kingdom', *Sociologie du Travail*, 47, 323–339.

Jansson, K (2007) *British Crime Survey: Measuring Crime for 25 Years* (London: Home Office).

Jones, G. and Levi, M. (2000) *The Value of Identity and the Need for Authenticity.* DTI Office of Science and Technology Crime Foresight Panel Essay for *Turning the Corner,* http://www.cf.ac.uk/sosci/resources/levi-identity.pdf, date accessed 29 May 2009.

Kahn, R. and Canell, C. (1957) *The Dynamics of Interviewing* (New York: John Wiley).

Kaplan, A. (1964) *The Conduct of Enquiry: Methodology for Behavioural Science* (San Francisco: Chandler).

Kaufman, D., Kraay, A. and Mastruzzi, M. (2006) *Measuring Corruption: Myths and Realities,* http://www1.worldbank.org/publicsector/anticorrupt/corecourse2007/ Myths.pdf, date accessed 15 January 2014.

Keenan, D. C. (2007) *Smith and Keenan's English Law: Text and Cases,* 15th edn (Harlow: Pearson Education Limited).

Kirk, D. (2008) 'Opinion: Fighting Fraud', *The Journal of Criminal Law*, 72, 335–337.

Kleinman, A., Yan, Y., Jun, J., Lee, S., Zhang, E., Tianshu, P., Fei, W. and Jinhua, G. (2011) *Deep China: The Moral Life of the Person, What Anthropology and Psychiatry Tell Us about China Today*) Berkeley, LA: University of California Press).

KPMG (2010) *Fraud Barometer.* http://www.kpmg.co.uk/email/01Jan10/183902/RRD_183902_Yorkshire_page2.html, date accessed 02 June 2012.

KPMG (2011) *Who is the Typical Fraudster?* (London: KPMG International).

KPMG (2012) *Fraud Barometer.* http://www.kpmg.com/uk/en/issuesandinsights/articlespublications/newsreleases/pages/fraud-barometer-boom-time-for-fraudsters-as-austerity-bites.aspx, date accessed 17 July 2012.

KPMG (2014) *Fraud Barometer.* http://www.kpmg.com/UK/en/IssuesAndInsights/ArticlesPublications/Documents/PDF/Latest%20

News/fraud-barometer-infographic-2014.PDF, date accessed 05 February 2014.

KROLL (2009) *Global Fraud Report: Annual Edition 2009/2010*. http://www.kroll.com/library/fraud/FraudReport_English-UK_Apr10.pdf, date accessed 22 June 2010.

KROLL (2014) *Global Fraud Report: Annual Edition 2013/2014*. http://fraud.kroll.com/wp-content/uploads/2013/10/ GlobalFraudReport_2013–14_WEB.pdf, date accessed 05 February 2014.

Levi, M. and Burrows, J. (2008) Measuring the Impact of Fraud in the UK: A Conceptual and Empirical Journey, *British Journal of Criminology*, 48, 293–318.

Levi, M., Burrows, J., Fleming, M. H. and Hopkins, M. (with the assistance of Matthews, K.) (2007) *The Nature, Extent and Economic Impact of Fraud in the UK* (London: ACPO).

Litvak, K. (2006) *The Effect of the Sarbanes–Oxley Act on Non–US Companies Cross–Listed in the US*, Law and Economics Research Paper No. 55 (Texas: University of Texas School of Law).

Livingstone, T. (2009) *Multi–Billion Pound Bank Bail–Out 'No Blank Cheque'*, http://www.walesonline.co.uk/news/wales-news/2009/01/20/multi-billion-pound-bank, date accessed 21 July 2010.

Maguire, M. (2007) 'Crime Data and Statistics' in M. Maguire, R. Morgan, and R. Reiner (eds) *The Oxford Handbook of Criminology*, 4th edn (Oxford: Oxford University Press), pp. 241–301.

Maguire, M. (2012) 'Criminal Statistics and the Construction of Crime' in M. Maguire, R. Morgan, and R. Reiner (eds) *The Oxford Handbook of Criminology*, 5th edn (Oxford: Oxford University Press), pp. 206–244.

Maxfield, M., Hough, M. and Mayhew, P. (2007) 'Surveying Crime in the 21st Century: Summary and Recommendations' in M. Hough and M. Maxwell (eds), *Surveying Crime in the 21st Century* (Cullompton: Willan), pp. 303–316.

Miller, W. L. (2006) 'Perceptions, Experience and Lies: What Measures Corruption and What do Corruption Measures Measure?', in C. Samford, A. Shacklock, C. Connors, and F. Galtung (eds), *Measuring Corruption* (Aldershot: Ashgate), pp. 163–185.

Ministry of Defence (2011) *New group set up to tackle crime against the Armed Forces*. http://www.mod.uk/DefenceInternet/ DefenceNews/ DefencePolicyAndBusiness/NewGroupSetUpToTackleCrimeAgainstTheArmedForces.htm, date accessed 21 June 2011.

DOI: 10.1057/9781137406286.0012

Ministry of Justice (2011) *The Bribery Act 2010: Quick Start Guide* (London: Ministry of Justice).

Mirrlees-Black, C. and Ross, A. (1995) *Crime against Retail and Manufacturing Premises: Findings from the 1994 Commercial Victimization Survey*, Home Office Research Study 146 (London: Home Office).

Mishcon de Reya (2005) *Protecting Corporate Britain from Fraud* (London: Mishcon de Reya).

Mistry, V. and Usherwood, R. C. (1996) Total Quality Management, British Standard accreditation, Investors In People and academic libraries. *Information Research*, 1(3), http://InformationR.net/ir/1–3/paper9.html, date accessed 24 June 2011.

Moeller, R. R. (2004) *Sarbanes Oxley and the New International Auditing Rules* (Hoboken, NJ: John Wiley and Sons).

Morse, J. M. (2003) 'Principles of Mixed Methods and Multimethod Research Design' in A. Tashakkori and C. Teddlie (eds) *Handbook of Mixed Methods in Social and Behavioural Research* (Thousand Oaks, CA: Sage), pp. 189–208.

Murphy, A., and Topyan, K. (2005) 'Corporate governance: a critical survey of key concepts, issues, and recent reforms in the US', *Employee Responsibilities and Rights Journal*, 17(2), 75–89.

Nardi, P. M. (2006) *Doing Survey Research: A Guide to Quantitative Methods,* 2nd edn (New York: Pearson).

National Audit Office (1998). *Appropriation Accounts 1996–97: Class XII, Vote 1-Central Government Administered Social Security Benefits and other payments.* London: The Stationary Office.

National Audit Office (2008a) *Department for Work and Pensions: Progress in Tackling Benefit Fraud.* Report by the Comptroller and Auditor General. HC102, Session 2007–2008 (London: The Stationery Office).

National Audit Office (2008b) *Good Practice in Tackling External Fraud* (London: National Audit Office).

National Commission on the Causes of the Financial and Economic Crisis in the United States (2011) *The Financial Crisis Inquiry Report* (USA: Pacific Publishing Studio).

National Economic Research Associates (2000) *The Economic Cost of Fraud*: *A Report for the Home Office and the Serious Fraud Office* (London: Home Office).

National Fraud Authority (NFA) (2009) Regional Fraud Summits, http://www.lslo.gov.uk/nfa/GuidetoInformation/Documents/NFA_Regional%20Fraud_Summits_Report_%20July_2009.pdf, date accessed 06 April, 2010

National Fraud Authority (2010a) *Annual Fraud Indicator*, http://www.attorneygeneral.gov.uk/nfa/GuidetoInformation/Documents/NFA_fraud_indicator.pdf, date accessed 06 May 2010.

National Fraud Authority (2010b) *Fraud Focus*. Edition 5, February 2010. http://www.attorneygeneral.gov.uk/nfa/WhatAreWeSaying/Documents/Fraud%20Focus_Ed_5_ED_FEB_2010.pdf, date accessed 06 May 2010.

National Fraud Authority (2011a) *Annual Fraud Indicator,* http://www.attorneygeneral.gov.uk/nfa/WhatAreWeSaying/Documents/AFI%202011.pdf, date accessed 27 May 2011.

National Fraud Authority (2011b) *Achievements in 2010/11nnual Fraud Indicator*, http://www.attorneygeneral.gov.uk/ nfa/WhatAreWeSaying/Documents/NFA%20an%20review%202011.pdf, date accessed 27 June 2011.

National Fraud Authority (2011c) *Fraud Focus*. Edition 11, February 2011, http://www.attorneygeneral.gov.uk/nfa/WhatAreWeSaying/Documents/FF%20Feb%202011.pdf, date accessed 06 May 2010.

National Fraud Authority (2012) *Annual Fraud Indicator* (London: National Fraud Authority).

National Fraud Authority (2013) *Annual Fraud Indicator* (London: National Fraud Authority).

National Fraud Strategic Authority (2008) *Business Plan 2008/09* (London: National Fraud Strategic Authority).

National Health Service (1999) *Countering Fraud in the NHS*, Wetherby: Department of Health).

National Health Service Counter Fraud and Security Management Service (2001a) *Countering Fraud in the NHS: Identifying the Nature and Scale of the Problem* (London: Department of Health).

National Health Service Counter Fraud and Security Management Service (2001b) *Countering Fraud in the NHS: Protecting your NHS* (London: Department of Health)

National Health Service Counter Fraud and Security Management Service (2007) *Countering Fraud in the NHS: Protecting Resources for Patients. 1999–2006 Performance Statistics* (NHSCFMS: London).

National Statistician (2011) *National Statistician's Review of Crime Statistics: England and Wales* (London: Office of National Statistics).

DOI: 10.1057/9781137406286.0012

Newburn, T. (2007) *Criminology* (Cullompton: Willan).

Nicholas, S., Kershaw, C. and Walker, A. (2007) *Crime in England and Wales 2006/07* (London: Home Office).

Norwich Union (2005) *The Fraud Report: Shedding Light on Hidden Crime* (Norwich: Norwich Union).

Office for National Statistics (2012) *Crime in England and Wales– Quarterly First Release, March 2012* (London: Office for National Statistics).

Payment Accuracy (n.d.) Success Stories, http://www.paymentaccuracy. gov/ content/success-stories, date accessed 25 February 2013.

Philips, L. (2010) *Fraud Experts Question Accuracy of Statistics*, http:// www.publicfinance.co.uk/news/2010/01/fraud-experts-question-accuracy-of-statistics/, date accessed 26 April 2010.

Politics.co.uk (2007) Darling Defends Northern Rock Bail–Out. 19 November, 2007, http://www.politics.co.uk/news/economy-and-finance/darling-defends-northern-rock-bail-out-$481758.htm, date accessed 16 August 2010.

PriceWaterhouseCoopers (2010) *Fraud in the Public Sector* (London: PriceWaterhouseCoopers).

PriceWaterhouseCoopers (2011) *Combating Cybercrime to Protect UK Organizations: Global Economic Crime Survey,* http://www.pwc.co.uk/ forensic-services/publications/global-economic-crime-survey-2011-uk-report.jhtml, date accessed 24 April 2013.

Reddy, W. and McCarthy, S. (2006) 'Sharing Best Practice', *International Journal of Health Care Quality Assurance,* 19(7), 504–598.

Reinikka, R. and Svensson, J. (2005) 'Using Micro Surveys to Measure and Explain Corruption', *World Development,* 34(2), 359–70.

Rohwer, A. (2009) *Measuring Corruption: A Comparison Between the Transparency International's Corruption Perceptions Index and the World Bank's Worldwide Governance Indicators,* https://www.cesifo-group.de/ DocDL/dicereport309-rr2.pdf, date accessed 24 February 2014.

RSM Robson Rodes (2004) *Economic Crime Survey* (London: RSM Robson Rodes).

Russell, N. (1998) *Dealing with Fraud: A Survey of UK Companies* (London: Neville Russell).

Sainsbury, R. (2003) 'Understanding Social Security Fraud' in J. Millar (ed.) *Understanding Social Security: Issues for Policy and Practice* (Bristol: Policy Press), pp. 277–295.

Samford, C., Shacklock, A., Connors, C. and Galtung, F. (eds) (2006), *Measuring Corruption* (Aldershot: Ashgate).

DOI: 10.1057/9781137406286.0012

Schick, A. (2007) *The Federal Budget: Politics, Policy, Process*, 3rd edn (Washington, DC: Brookings Institution Press).

Shury, J., Speed, M., Vivian, D., Kuechel, A. and Nicholas, S. (2005) *Crime against Retail and Manufacturing Premises: Findings from the 2002 Commercial Victimization Survey* (London: Home Office).

Sutherland, E. H. (1940) 'White Collar Criminality', *American Sociological Review*, 5, 1–12.

Sutherland, E. H. and Cressey, D. R. (1960) *Principles of Criminology* (Philadelphia: Lippincott).

Sutton, M. (2007) 'Improving National Crime Surveys: With a Focus Upon Strangely Neglected Offenders and Their Offences, Including Fraud, High–Tech Crimes, and Handling Stolen Goods' in M. Hough and M. Maxwell (eds) *Surveying Crime in the 21st Century* (Cullompton: Willan), pp. 243–261.

Tackett, J., Woolf, F. and Claypole, G. (2004) 'Sarbanes–Oxley and Audit Failure: A Critical Examination', *Managerial Auditing Journal*, 19(3), 340–350.

Tashakkori, A. and Teddlie, C. (1998) *Mixed Methodology: Combining Qualitative and Quantitative Approaches*. Applied Social Research Methods 46 (Thousand Oaks CA: Sage).

Thomas, D. and Loader, B. D. (eds) (2003) *Cyber Crime* (London: Routledge).

Transparency International (2013) *Global Corruption Barometer 2013*, http://www.transparency.org/whatwedo/pub/global_corruption_ barometer_2013, date accessed 25 February 2014.

Trickett, J. (2010) *George Osborne's Cuts Risk Economic Death Spiral*. http://www.guardian.co.uk/commentisfree/2010/may/17/george- osborne-austerity-measures/print, date accessed 12 August 2010.

Tunley, M. (2010a) Uncovering the Iceberg: Mandating the Measurement of Fraud in the United Kingdom, *International Journal of Law, Crime and Justice (2010)*, xx, doi:10.1016/j.ijlcj.2011.05.007, http://www.sciencedirect. com/science/article/pii/S1756061611000541, date accessed 21 June 2011.

Tunley, M. (2010b) Need, Greed or Opportunity? An Examination of who Commits Benefit Fraud and Why They Do It. *Security Journal*, Advance Online Publication, 15 November 2010, 1–18, http://www. palgrave-journals.com/sj/journal/vaop/ncurrent/abs/sj20105a.html, date accessed 21 June 2011.

DOI: 10.1057/9781137406286.0012

Tunley, M. (2011) 'Counterblast: Another Case of Old Wine in New Bottles? The Coalition's Misguided Strategy to Reduce Benefit Fraud', *The Howard Journal of Criminal Justice*, 50(3), 314–317.

TV Licensing (2009) *Delivering more for Less* (TV Licensing: Bristol).

United Nations Development Programme (2008) *A User's Guide to Measuring Corruption* (Oslo: United Nations Development Programme).

United States Department of Agriculture (2002) *Performance and Accountability Report FY 2002*, http://www.ocfo.usda.gov/usdarpt/par2002/pdf/par2002.pdf, date accessed 02 May 2013.

United States Department of Agriculture (2003) *Annual Report for Fiscal Year 2003: Report on Performance and Accountability*, http://www.ocfo.usda.gov/ usdarpt/par2003/pdf/par2003.pdf, date accessed 02 May 2013.

United States Department of Agriculture (2004) *Performance and Accountability Report FY 2004*, http://www.ocfo.usda.gov/usdarpt/par2004/pdf/par2004.pdf, date accessed 02 May 2013.

United States Energy and Commerce Committee Subcommittee on Health (2012) *Hearing on Examining Options to Combat Health Care Waste, Fraud and Abuse*, November 28, 2012 (Washington: US Energy and Commerce Committee).

United States General Accounting Office (2001) *Strategies to Manage Improper Payments: Learning from Public and Private Sector Organizations*. http://www.gao.gov/new.items/d0269g.pdf, date accessed 30 July 2010.

United States Government Accountability Office (2012) *Improper Payments: Remaining Challenges and Strategies for Governmentwide Reduction Efforts*. GAO–12–573T. Washington: The United States Government Accountability Office.

United States Office of Management and Budget (2003) *Implementation Guidance for the Improper Payments Information Act of 2002. PL 107–300*, http://www.whitehouse.gov/sites/default/files/omb/assets/omb/memoranda/m03-13-attach.pdf, date accessed 09 August 2010.

United States Office of Management and Budget (2006) Requirements for Effective Measurement and Remediation of Improper Payments, Appendix C to OMB Circular A–123, http://www.whitehouse.gov/omb/circulars/ a123/a123_appx-c.pdf, date accessed 30 July 2010.

United States Office of Management and Budget (2010) *Memorandum for Heads of Executive Departments and Agencies, M–10–13*, http://www.

whitehouse.gov/omb/assets/a123/a123_appx-c.pdf, date accessed 06 June 2010

Van Dijk, J. J. M. (2012) *Closing the Doors: Highlights of the International Crime Victims Survey 1987–2012, Valedictory Lecture* (Tilburg: Tilburg University).

von Solms, B. (2000) 'Information Security–The Third Wave?', *Computers and Security*, 19, 615–620.

Walker, S. (2011) *Sense and Nonsense about Crime, Drugs, and Communities* (7th edn) (Belmont, CA: Wadsworth).

Walters, R. (2005) 'Boycott, Resistance and the Role of the Deviant Voice', *Criminal Justice Matters*, 62(1), 6–7.

Wilson, D., Patterson, A., Powell, G. and Hembury, R. (2006) *Fraud and Technology Crimes: Findings from the 2003/04 British Crime Survey, the 2004 Offending Crime and Justice Survey and Administrative Sources* (London: Home Office).

Words and Phrases (1959) *Words and Phrases* (Minnesota: West Publishing Company).

Wyant, C. (2003) Executive Certification Requirements in the Sarbanes–Oxley Act of 2002: A Case for Criminalizing Effective Recklessness', *Seattle University Law Review*, 27, 561–584.

DOI: 10.1057/9781137406286.0012

Index

Action Fraud, 31
Association of British Insurers, 19, 43, 55, 61, 67,110
Association of Chief Police Officers (ACPO), 44
Audit Commission, 3, 37, 38, 55, 58, 59, 61, 115, 124
Protecting the Public Purse, 38
Auditing Practices Board, 20
average fraud loss figure, 22–25, 49, 53

bank charges, 122
banking crisis, 21–23, 27, 120
banking fraud, 19
banking industry, 18, 65, 85, 102, 103, 108
banks,
    government bailout of, 21–23, 27
BDO, 46, 55, 57, 61, 120
    Fraud Track, 46
benefit fraud, 23, 31
best practice, developing, 10, 13, 19, 20, 26, 37, 54, 60, 69, 78, 102, 108–110, 127
Braithwaite, John, 122, 123, 125
Bribery Act 2010, 26, 27, 120
British Banking Association, 98
British Broadcasting Corporation, 23, 39, 55, 61
British Crime Survey, 31

British standard of fraud measurement, 10, 14, 19–20, 24, 88, 94, 101–107, 110, 116, 117, 121, 123, 125–127
British Standard 10500, 27
British Standards Institute, 20, 27
British Standards Institution, 19
Brown, Gordon, 21
Bush, President George W, 26

Cabinet Office, 39, 58, 69, 123, 124, 125
    Fraud, Error and Debt Taskforce, 33, 60, 83, 118, 122, 125
charitable sector, 5, 12, 47, 52–53, 64, 74, 89, 107, 114–115
Charity Commission, 52, 53
Child and Working Tax Credits, 42
CIFAS, 43, 61
Fraudscape, 52
civil aspects of fraud, 3
Commercial Victimization Survey, 31, 32, 34
control strategies, *see* counter fraud strategies
corruption, 69
    definition, 6
    measuring, 6–8

146

DOI: 10.1057/9781137406286.0013

Lightning Source UK Ltd.
Milton Keynes UK
UKOW03n1325300414

230867UK00002B/4/P